Messages from the Divine

With

Answers

Printed and bound in the UK by

Biddles
Castle House
East Winch Road
Blackborough End
King's Lynn
Norfolk PE32 1SF

Registered at Nielsen

A catalogue copy of this book available from the British library

ISBN
978-1-913218-22-5

The Rules for being Human

handed down from ancient Sanskrit

You will receive a body

you may like it or not, but it will be yours for the entire period round.

You will learn lessons

You are enrolled in a full-time, informal school called life. Each day in this school you will have the opportunity to learn lessons. You may like the lessons or think them irrelevant and stupid

There are no mistakes, only lessons

Growth is a process of trial and error, experimentation. The failed experiments are as much a part of the process as the experiment that ultimately works.

A lesson is repeated until it is learned

A lesson will be presented to you in various forms until you have learned it, then you can go on to the next lesson

Learning lessons does not end
There is no part of life that does not contain its lessons. If you are alive there are lessons to be learned.

There is no better than here
When your `there` has become `here` you will simply obtain another `there` that will, again look better then `here`

Others are merely mirrors of you
You cannot love or hate something about another person unless it reflects to you something you love or hate about yourself.

What you make of your life is up to you
You have all the tools and resources you need, what you do with them is up to you. The choice is yours

The answers lie inside you
The answers to life's questions lie inside you. All you need to do is look, listen and trust

Forward

This was as you can see by the date at the beginning written back in January 1992 and was given to me by what is known in spiritual terms as automatic writing and thought while being unaware of what you are writing.

This is a "TRUTH". I have never played with anyone's mind or their emotions. I have never been money or ego motivated. I don't do websites, business cards, private readings, or promote myself. I have been a spiritual medium for some years but in truth not knowing it. I only serve churches and there are churches here in Scotland that have never even heard about me and here is another TRUTH, it is not about me. If the divine and Spirit want you to help someone then They will make it happen!

There is no such thing as Coincidence it is a message from the Divine without a signature.

Some years ago, they set me up to go and do a community radio station where they gave me the Healing Slot which went out across the world wide net. After leaving it they once again came to me and said we want you to start it up on face book which is currently up and running and brings Healing, Love and Hugs to those in need.

The Greatest gift you can give another human being is of yourself your Love and Forgiveness without ever looking for anything in return

This was given to me some 24 years ago and although at the time I never really understood why! I knew deep within there is a reason for everything that happens to you in your life time.
Over many weeks and months, the divine would have me sit down and write some more, then one day it was finished.
My community psychiatric nurse who would visit me after recovering from my nervous breakdown would often ask what I was writing and I could only reply at the time "I don't know"
He asked when it was finished would I read some of it to him, my reply was I don't think it would be interesting and left it at that.

Months after it was finished, he visited me one day out of the blue and said I thought I would pop in for a cuppa and see if you have finished the book! I said yes, I have but I feel after reading it for the first time it is for my children, for them to understand the man behind the man they saw as their Father! So I don't think you would find it of any interest to you. He nevertheless asked if I would read him some of it and after reading him some of it, said "Wow" you really don't know how that could help a lot of people! I thought he was being "Nice" and duly put it away forgetting about it till I received a spiritual Message back at the beginning of 2015 some 23 years later.

The message was simple, dig out the book and the divine realms will give not only you answers but will answer a lot of questions for many others. They will change the text so people understand it is the divine giving the answers and not what you think is a Truth. Although this has taken some 23 years later for the divine to make me read it again and then insert at the right times and points and questions that have not only opened my eyes and gave me answers I know it will also give you the answers you have been searching a lifetime for.

You can be the judge after reading it.

Love Casper. X

Sunday 5th January 1992, 8:34am.

Sitting writing in bed listening to Simply Red "I want to fall from the stars straight into your arms, I hope you comprehend".
I am asking you all if you comprehend? Can't really say that I comprehend what is happening because I, like most people, take life on face value. Wanting to push myself to the very limits that life allows you to but never quite achieving success. How does one measure success in terms of a big house? big car? and lots of money? Well, I thought life was about all of the above, but it has taken me 30 and a bit years to comprehend that life as we understand it at this point in our growth of learning stage, that contentment, peace of mind is far more important to our soul than all the money in the world.

To be at peace with one's mind, and never underestimate the power of the mind, it is probably next to nuclear weapons, the most powerful thing we possess. These events as I am about to detail are actually events that happened in my life. I for one can only grow and learn from experiences.
It is from these very experiences that I want to share with you.
I am, in doing so, setting myself up to the learned people in our society. And of course with the learned people, come the narrow minded who do not comprehend and even though the events are accurate and did happen, these people who do not understand what is really happening around them will never for reasons of their own, be it fear, uncertainty, lack of knowledge, never face the truth and the reason I write this is dedicated to them.

When you understand Death is not the end
It allows the Mind to continue its Journey Where
Lessons have to be learned but more importantly
have to be understood

May I take you back 30 years ago, when I was 5? I, like most people, was a happy, healthy, normal child. My parents were like most, worked very hard to bring us up on very small wages. There was nothing startling in that, because most families around at the time experienced the exact same thing.

We were in my eyes, a very close family. I would play outside, always on the go, back and forward running up and down playing with my cat. How I loved that little furry creature, so innocent, independent, playful, my own little friend. Around the corner from where I lived, on the corner house, was a little dog that when I went past would always bite my heels. I asked and asked my mother, pleading with her to buy me a pair of wellingtons. Not unusual you may say, but in the middle of summer it is an unusual request, but this request was of no great importance at that time, or so I thought, but I was to discover 30 years later that it was very important.

I was being sent to Church every Sunday. I was brought up a Roman Catholic. My mother would turn me out immaculately, iron my shirt, press my trousers and off I would go in all innocence to the Church. At the time, in truth, I did not really understand it all but I, like most children, listened to my mother and father as the years rolled by. And they do. As I write this it is as though I am still there. The memory is so clear that without a doubt it is only like a few hours ago.

We had neighbours starting to spring up all around us as our house was the first to be built. We were in a block of two, the neighbours became friends. Next door to us was Mr and Mrs Archibald who, like my mother and father, had two boys and one girl. Jim was my friend.

They lived in number 64 we lived next door at 66. One up at 68 was Mr and Mrs Niven. And staying in number 70 was Mr and Mrs Bryce. They had a son and a daughter. Harry was my friend. His sister Marette was very beautiful and I suppose like most kids I had a crush on her. She was and still is a very attractive woman.

Onto no. 72, were Mr and Mrs Main lived, they had three children, two boys and a girl. John was also a friend. Next door to them were Mr and Mrs Blair at number 74, and finally next door at 76 were Mr and Mrs Walker. Their son Ian made up the “famous 5”.

We spent summers going to the outdoor swimming pool in Saltcoats. Also. we were all blessed with having the shore on our doorstep where we would also go down to look for small fish and crabs under the rocks.
We would also go up the country to seek adventures in the forest and spend all day there, we would take sandwiches, crisps and juice which was usually Creamola foam in an empty ginger bottle. (Creamola Foam was a soft drink produced in the form of soluble crystals. It was manufactured in Glasgow and sold mainly in Scotland from the 1950s until Nestlé ended production in October 1998).

Every Sunday I would go along to the Church. The bible formed or what seemed at the time to form, a large part of my life, both in the Church and also at school, even more so at school. It appeared to me that it was the only important learning event in the education system.

In between all this learning and growing, Mr and Mrs Cook who lived just around the corner were becoming part of our lives. They had a daughter Elizabeth. I could not remember her name there but it suddenly flashed into my mind. Anyway, Mrs Cook was very involved in the Church, raising funds, helping at galas, fêtes etc. My sister Helen used to go shopping for Mr Cook as Mrs Cook was always involved in the Church. I started to get to know Mr Cook as he had a car, a Vauxhall Zodiac, he was always working on it, and I was interested in cars. He would teach me what he was doing and even take me out for a drive, which was not unusual as I had the same friendship with Mr Hilton across the road. Both said they liked me because I was always polite, courteous and always willing to learn.

My thirst for knowledge given the fact that at school I was not considered to be bright, let alone even considered average never stopped me in my quest for the truth! Time passed as it always does, the next event that happened was to change my life completely. At the time I would not understand it, but it would be made clear some 20 years later. Anyway, Mrs Cook ran off with the local Priest. As you can imagine, this was to have a devastating effect on Mr Cook. He would go and get blind drunk. I never saw Mr Cook one Saturday, when I called there was no answer. I never really thought about it at the time

Sunday came, and I went around to see him, again no reply. I waited for another hour, went back round, still no reply. I was just about to climb on the coal bunker and look in the window when my Mum came out of the back door to hang her washing out.

She called out to me “Bobby, get off that bunker, its bad manners to look into people's windows”. I literally became very cold from head to toe and said to my mother “Mum, something has happened to Mr Cook” She said “what do you mean?” I said “I don't know it's a feeling I have”. She then said “it's alright son, he's fine, and he’s probably gone to his brother Stephens for the weekend”

We were aware that Mr Cook had passed many hours before and on his request we intervened as he did not want you to suffer any distress in seeing him in this way as he knew how sensitive you were and knew this would have had a long term adverse effect on you. We were walking with you daily and that is how you felt cold from head to toe. Because everything happens for a reason and you would be given the answers as your life progressed.

Stephen came up on the Monday. I said I hadn't seen Mr Cook and was very worried. I was going to the shops at the time for a paper for my dad. We had this conversation on the corner of Burns Avenue. I went for the paper, came back over the road only to find a lot of activity around about Mr Cook's home. I asked my mother what was happening. My sister was crying. Mr Cook had committed suicide. I never discussed this with anyone until now but I felt if I had disobeyed my Mum on that Sunday, I would have managed to save him. He was a good man.

After that I lost interest in the Church, which was most surprising to me as I wanted to train to become a Priest. I suppose, on reflection, it was a reaction to the events that had taken place. One has to understand that for every action there is a reaction, but at that time in my life I did not understand.

We react to what in truth is only part of a truth. But the truth is there for everyone to find!

Time passed, and before I knew it, I was at secondary school. Still it appeared that religion was the dominating feature of the school curriculum. I met a girl called Catherine, fell in love, I hear you say "and lived happily ever after". Wrong! We were engaged. I had started my trade as a chef having left school at 15, having left in the schools eyes as an "idiot". The teachers said I would be a dustbin man. That thought has remained in my life all these years. People just don't understand that words are exceptionally powerful and can hurt and scar a person for life, now you have been made aware of this choose your words more carefully

Anyway, I started work and Catherine started as a waitress. She started to come in later than expected, which in itself was no big deal, but her mother and father never really approved of me because I wasn't going to the church and they were church goers. It was when Catherine started to come in with love bites that I knew things were starting to fall apart. We would have rows after which she pleaded with me not to tell her mum. I found myself lying to her Mum, that I was to blame for the marks on her neck. God, did I take some stick for that. She went to work in a new area as a waitress, which was in many ways a way to either move forward and get our relationship back on track or not and in truth I did not really understand what was happening.

We the Divine will take you out of a situation when the Lesson has been delivered. As Humans you fight against change but the secret is to embrace the change because with change comes wisdom but more importantly, your soul growth, which is the reason why you are all here!

I got a phone call from her Mum to inform me she had been involved in a car accident. Her Mum in my mind was unaware our relationship was in turmoil, nevertheless I went with her mum to see her. Again, I thought on the way down in the car, if I was not so possessive and paranoid about a couple of love bites, I would not have started this chain reaction that had resulted in her accident.

We arrived after a long car journey. Her face was badly bruised and swollen. I held her in my arms and asked her to come back to her Mothers and we would pick up the pieces. She said “Robert, I think I am pregnant, don't tell my Mum please”.

On the way back up the road on that long journey her mum said "what's up Robert? You are very quiet". I said "Oh, nothing" and just sat deep in thought. When I got home, I lay awake all night trying to solve the problem because the other fundamental thing in life is 'for every problem there is a solution'. It came eventually!

I phoned the next day and said to Catherine "do you love this man? She said "I don't know, why?" I replied "let's say to your Mum it is my baby and I will bring it up as my own", But it was not to be. She said that she would marry this man. I left, heartbroken and decided to run away from the nightmare.

A major Lesson you failed to understand at the time was by running away would only impact and make the problem of facing the Truth not only more difficult but would lead to many years of mind anguish.

I went to work in St Albans at the Noke Hotel. Again, it was a learning curve, on my own, no friends, no-one to share my anxiety, my fears with.
At the time of writing this I never realised back then that this was supposed to be my time to learn lessons but I knew there was a change in me happening that I could not understand. Again God puts the lessons in front of you… it is up to you to be aware and recognise what you are being shown because the truth is all the reasons and answers are starring you right in the face
But when your mind is in turmoil you cannot see what is in fact the mind that is the problem. If I had faced up to it and asked for the help, I in truth needed, I would have saved myself many years of mental anguish. But again, it is about understanding yourself and facing the truth about yourself and until you are ready to face the truth your life will be a roller coaster of highs and lows.
But there may be more lows than highs! Most of my

time was taken up with work and I used to work my days off if I could. Another fine example of burying ones head in the sand. On my days I would take off I would go into town and walk about aimlessly spending a lot of time in McDonald's eating my favourite chicken nuggets and curry sauce dip washed down with a strawberry milkshake. I would also spend time going to the cinema in St Albans and would go to London for the day and take in a theatre show. I tried to get into the Mouse Trap but it was booked solid and the lady said to me I have a reduced ticket to see Max Wall. I thought well I might as well so off I went and he was performing his one man show. As I sat there in front of this funny man who would be very funny and then sit down on the stage to share his life. It had me in tears, as here was a man that had given joy and laughter to thousands and yet he was so deeply unhappy within himself. A lesson was being shown to me once again, but again it would be many years in the future that I was to learn it and that lesson is simply this,

Life is an illusion

I would visit my sister on an occasion and as she stayed in Willesden gave me somewhere different to go and also it was a link to my family. St. Albans is a very affluent area I was in a music shop one day just having a look and killing a bit of time when a gentleman walked in, none other than the hairy monster Dave Lee Travis from radio 1. I used to love listening to him. I will never forget that I wanted to tell him that but was like a rabbit caught in the headlamps and just stared with my mouth open with a daft look on my face. He quipped, you better shut your mouth or you will catch flies… and with that he was gone! I never did get the chance to say hello and thank him for all the great music he played and I could relate to. As I left the shop, I was aware of a homeless person, an old man looking on the ground for cigarette ends and although I was in the middle of St Albans and yes it was very affluent it was as though he did not exist. I walked past him and then something inside made me turned back. I went into a newsagents and bought him a packet of 10 cigarettes and handed them to him. I spent the rest of that day and in fact many months and years thinking I should have bought him a meal instead of a cancer stick. Again, another lesson that has taken many years of understanding. That is how complex we as humans really are and how complex the mind is!

Next to nuclear weapons your mind is the most powerful thing you possess many here fail to understand and underestimate the power of the mind.

I moved a few months later to a little place called Whittlesey near Peterborough. I met a lovely girl called Janet; she was introduced to me by a woman that worked in the kitchen beside me. I asked her if she would like to go to the pictures in Peterborough she said "yes" and off we went. This was my first relationship after my engagement. She was a stunning looking girl and I thought at the time what could I offer her? Yet another lesson should have been learned… and that was just enjoy the moment and don't think too deeply. I suppose on reflection that was my problem, I always thought to deep. We went and had a great time, I remember very clearly, we had missed the bus and had to wait till the last bus which got into Whittlesey later than she had told her Mum. As we got off in the town centre, we really did not care about the time we were so wrapped up in each other's company but as we came round the corner her Mum Peggy was out looking for her worried out her mind. I apologised to her Mum but she was sick with worry and took Janet's hand and returned home. As I was walking back to the hotel where I worked and lived in, I was tormented by the fact that I had such a wonderful time with Janet but I had deeply let her

Mum down. The following morning I went to the local florist and bought a bouquet of flowers with a card and sent them to her Mum I said on the card "I am so sorry for all the worry I caused you and it was my fault we missed the bus".

I was invited to tea and met her Dad Ted I felt really at home with the whole Family Janet's Mother Loved me and wanted me to marry her daughter and she would say so on many different occasions. I could not see then what her Mum saw in me maybe it was the respect the honesty that I showed them but that was the way my Mother and Father had brought me up so to me it was natural. Soon after this I was transferred to another hotel within the group which was the Old Bridge Hotel in Huntingdon. I was by this time working all hours, not taking days off, not eating properly. I collapsed outside on my way from the changing room to the kitchen and was taken to hospital in Huntingdon.
After I had regained consciousness about two days later, a psychiatrist saw me. I was fuming mad? Get me back to the ward I demanded! I got out and started work again but I could not settle. After Janet my girlfriend and her Mum came to see me in hospital and said we have a spare room why not come and stay with us. Her Mum really enjoyed my company as did her Dad Ted.
So, I moved back to Whittlesey and eventually got myself another job. Her family showed me kindness by giving me a room to stay in and one night when her Mother and Father went to bed we started kissing and cuddling. We lay on the couch together fully clothed. I got overexcited and although fully clothed I knew she could feel I was excited. That had a devastating effect on me. I felt I had betrayed their very kindness. I left the following morning, went to a park and slashed my wrists, not in attempt to kill myself, but more a cry for help. You do not sit in a public park and cut your wrists, particularly on a Sunday. Anyway, I left, I felt totally disgusted with myself that I got overexcited and I felt that I had betrayed her Mother and Fathers trust.
What I did not realise was this extreme action was due to my engagement to Catherine finishing. If I had taken the doctors help, I may have saved myself many years of unhappiness.
Never be too proud to ask for help. I wish I had learned that lesson then.

One in three people will face mental health conditions in their life time, fact!

Asking for help is not easy and we know that!! but by asking for help it is the key that opens the door to facing the Truth about yourself which not only raises awareness but lets you understand that everything happens for a reason and Lessons have to be learnt but more importantly understood and once this is learned we can blend with you more easily and help you and give you a greater understanding which will enable you to complete your souls task thus fulfilling its purpose.

Anyway, I went to my sister and she said "Don't let mum or dad know about this. You can stay here until you get yourself sorted out". She tended to my wounds and loved me enough to take care of me. Weeks went by and I came back to Scotland. I started back to work in 1974 in Kilmarnock Infirmary as a Cook. It is here my life was to take on a totally new meaning. I met a girl at a nurse's party. Her name was Mary Banks. This woman was to become my wife. I would learn from her in terms of her serene and compassionate nature but I was blind and did not see until sadly for me it was too late, but! It is never too late to learn. We all must experience pain to learn by discussion, pre-death visions, near death experiences and death itself with dying patients and their families; we can take grief out of isolation and stop ignoring this difficult, yet inevitable event.

The words of Psychotherapist Carl Young spring to mind, and he said…
"We should not pretend to understand the world only by the intellect. We apprehend it just as much by feeling. Therefore, the judgement of the intellect is at best only half the truth".

Mary and I started to go out, nothing serious, but I was becoming more aware of feelings I was experiencing, excitement at the thought of meeting her. We did all the things that any normal young couple do; going out to the pictures, going for a drink and going for a meal.

About six months into the relationship things took a dramatic turn. I was asking at work for courses, in particular management courses. There was a new lad started in the kitchen. His name was Campbell Hewitson, a very brash outspoken lad. He had come from the Merchant Navy and every second word seemed like a swear word. He rubbed a lot of people up the wrong way but even I knew then, that although wild, you would always know where you stood with him. We eventually became friends. We went to a nurse's party and that's where I met Mary. Soon after that we went for a meal with Campbell and Janet who was his girlfriend at the time. They are now man and wife and what a lucky man I am to have been blessed and privileged to have their friendship all these years. You see, in many respects, we take so much for granted; each other, friends, people round about us, flowers, birds, all animals becoming aware is so much more about understanding and seeing what can't be seen.

I may not have the opportunity when I pass to thank each and every person that I have met, or people that have touched my life, even if it has only been a conversation on a train, a boat or in the supermarket. I would just like to applaud each and every one. My life has been truly enriched from all the experiences I have gained from you all.

As I said earlier, life was to take a dramatic turn. Campbell was put on a butchers course. I was very upset because I had been asking for a course for so long. I went to the Catering Officer to complain but she was not interested. I said to myself "I will show you". So, I saw a job advertised down South for trainee management couples. I went down for the interview myself without telling anyone, not even Mary. They said I was just what they were looking for but they were looking to take on couples and did I have a partner i.e. wife. I said "no" as Mary was married and separated, but they said girlfriend would be okay. I came back and asked Mary if she would be interested. She said "I don't know". I guess on reflection I could not blame her for being cautious as her marriage had been disastrous but I said come along for the interview anyway, and then decide.

We went down to the Rising Sun at Twickenham and got offered the job. We told our parents and before we knew it we went to start a new job, a new life together. The branch we were allocated to was the Crooked Billet in Staines in Middlesex. I will never forget arriving. Mary and I were soaked to the skin. We arrived wet, bedraggled, tired and hungry, but with an intense excitement about what lay ahead of us. We were introduced to the Manager, Bob Lewis-Jones, who said I will run you both to the Management House where you can get sorted out. I will pick you both up later and we will have a meal together. I knew instantly this was a good man, an honest, fair man. Why did I know that you may ask? I must say honestly that I did not know the answer to that question. The answer lay years ahead.

Life was hectic, working very long hours for very little pay. It seemed hardly worth the effort but from my heart I was enjoying it so much, although it was hard Mary was working every bit as hard as I was but was struggling with the long hours. We would quarrel. I went to my sisters in Basingstoke to get away from the very long hours and the rows. Mary phoned and asked what the matter was but in truth I did not really know. Was it the long hours? Was it the rows?

We got back together. Mary wanted to start a family.
But did not realise that was impossible in the license trade, so we came back to Scotland and started all over again. We both got jobs as bus conductors. We worked seven days and worked double shifts, which enabled us to buy a flat in Saltcoats overlooking the harbour. I remember the very first night Mary and I spent in our new home. A bed with just a very light quilt which we had bought at an auction on the day previous at the Erskine Bridge Hotel which cost us three pounds. It was very thin but at the time we were just so excited about moving in to our first home together. But the immense love that was running through my whole body was, and still is today, so very immense. I cannot find sufficient words to describe to you how wonderful, what this lady means to me. It was summed up the other day while walking in Irvine.
An acquaintance stopped me and said simply "Robert we have not forgotten Mary, everybody that knew her loved her". What can one say in reply to that? For my part I knew she was telling me what I already knew.
For all that I told Mary every day that I loved her I was bearing my very heart and soul in a way I had never really exposed before and now I am bearing my whole self to whoever picks this book up and reads it.

My hope is that in sharing this it will answer some questions you may have running around in your mind and in fact have had for many Years.
I do not feel ashamed or embarrassed to reveal what in essence is the real me. We all must change our outlook, not on short term goals but in a broader long term for the very survival of our future and if this means one person takes the time to read this and say to themselves

"I must make a start and be honest with myself and understand myself",

then I suppose they will also come to the conclusion and realisation that life should not and is not a vain struggle but a challenge to overcome.

The obstacles that are put before us are lessons to learn and more importantly understand and if while doing so, you unleash this deep love within, you will quickly understand that you have bought for yourselves something in the world that cannot be bought at any price. What is this great prize?
It is simply peace of mind. You see, life is like a gigantic jigsaw, when emptied out onto the table it looks daunting but suddenly you find a small corner piece and slowly but surely you start to build a picture. Now this picture may be revealed to some sooner and to others later, but the truth is the picture is there to behold for everyone. The sad fact is for many the truth never dawns on them until it is too late to see what was always in front of them.
But like many, we all get caught up in our own pleasures. Our pleasure was working all hours God allowed us to thus enabling us to buy our first flat in Windmill Street, Saltcoats, but you know life's material pleasures never in truth really last.
Mary and I enjoyed our work which inevitably led to the money which allowed us to enjoy the pleasures i.e. going out for a meal, to the pictures, buying what we wanted for the house, having the money to basically do what we wanted but alas there was something in both our lives missing.
I hear you ask "what could possibly be missing in their lives. They had their own flat, money to do as they pleased, what else could they need?" A child is what we needed and soon Mary was expecting our first child.
Mary worked as long as she could on the buses and when she had to stop we missed the money. I continued on the buses working all the overtime I could get and we were coping well enough.

The great day finally arrived; 6th March 1977 our daughter took her first breath. I was present at the birth to give my love and my support. You see, although apprehensive at the birth, how could I not attend the pinnacle of the love we had shared with each other resulting in Gods very special gift to both of us. The excitement running through me as I write this is as clear as it was in 1977. This was an experience that no man should ever miss. The pain Mary and many other women go through in birth is an explosion of the love they have for you

The old saying creeps into my mind 'no pain no gain'. It may sound quite contrite but very true. The gain is you have hopefully a healthy boy or girl. Once again, we take so much for granted but nothing in life are certain except for death, but death I will cover much later, or should I say I will cover continuation of life later. Any way you can decide for yourself.

After leaving the maternity section at Irvine Central I came back to the flat sitting there crying, drinking a cup of tea, listening to "Isn't she beautiful" by David Parton on Radio Luxembourg.
I wondered how I would cope as a father. How would this affect our lives? The reality had set in. I was scared

Karen arrived in her new home like most babies requiring attention, crying a lot, feeding, changing, and sleeping. This was another learning curve for both Mary and I. Everything was going fine until a bombshell was to be dropped on me at work, still a bus conductor with Western Buses in Princess Street, Ardrossan. We were informed that it was to be only a one-man operated service. Bus conductors were being paid off, but if you had a driving licence they would put you through your PSV (Passenger service vehicle), in short a bus driving licence.
I had not passed a car test so I was ruled out. I was worried sick about what effect this would have on Mary and my daughter. My mind was in turmoil. The fateful day came when I lost my job. The world seemed to collapse. Money was a state benefit. Not only was this not enough to survive on but the total indignity of having to sign on.

The system seemed to be totally inept of understanding a person's feelings of rejection, anger, dismay, the total humiliation of not having a purpose, in a working context I mean, led to the inevitable strain that was to overtake the relationship to the extent that we lost the real reason and purpose. The ability to think clearly and realise that you both had each other and a healthy baby. That, unfortunately, gets lost in the materialistic world we live in.

The rows were becoming constant. Mary threw Karen's glass feeding bottle at me. I snapped and ordered them out of the house. It was in my name because we were not married. She refused saying "you will get the police before I move". I did just that. Of all the experiences I have had in my life, this one action still reoccurs in my mind. I was, and still am, so sorry for that action. I now know that you can never change something once you have done it. I was watching the woman whom I loved walk away with my daughter in her arms.
It is still so fresh in my memory; I can never erase it.

You have learned that making mistakes is the very thing that enriches the soul as long as you learn the lesson and don't repeat the same mistake! you will reach an understanding that many only dream of understanding.

After a couple of weeks, Mary and baby were back. To say I was relieved was an understatement. I got a job back at my trade which was a chef. I went to work at Sullom Voe on the Shetland Islands as night shift baker. This was to be my first working away from home experience and to be perfectly honest one I did not relish. Even more so when you are stuck in a cabin in the wilderness with one phone and some 3,000 men. I could never get near the phone. I received a letter to say Mary was in hospital with a lump on her breast and Karen was taken into Irvine Central with a virus. I was sick with worry and flew home. I told Mary I did not want to leave her and Karen ever again as I wanted to take care of them and be there for them as I loved them more than anything in the world.

I was offered a move to Benbecula as Head Cook. Three weeks on, one off. Mary said that would be better, against my better judgement I took it but not for long. Back home in Saltcoats with very little job prospects Mary and I sat down to discuss our future and what we would do.

I was getting a catering magazine and saw a job as cook in a psychiatric hospital advertised, the one catch though the hospital was in Cambridge. Before we knew it, we arrived in Cambridge and I started work. The head cook took an instant dislike to me as he never employed me. The new catering manager did, and what I did not know at that time, the head cook thought he was going to be the next catering officer.

The politics were incredible; one would tell you one thing and then the other something completely different. It came to a head one day in the kitchen. The head cook wanted me to put curry out as spaghetti bolognaise to the patients. He said perhaps some of them would not know the difference because they have mental health problems. I was totally incensed by this and told him they deserved to be treated with respect. I refused to be a party to this and promptly walked out of the kitchen to the famous words of 'Scottish Bastard' ringing in my ears.

I told Mary what had happened expecting to be told off as Mary was working in the hospital across from me working with mentally/hyperactive kids as a domestic.
I said "I know you have a right to be angry with me". We were in a tied house and I walked out but these people deserve respect and love. Mary just looked at me and said "You did the right thing". Yes, I did but I was to suffer at the tribunal as they said I should have done as I was told. I simply said "When you lose your respect, compassion for your fellow human, who is less fortunate in life than you are, then it is time to take stock of your own purpose in life".
Again, it was me who put Mary and Karen after my own personal morals but I never meant that to happen. God how I wish Mary could know that.

We were testing "you" to see if you understood the importance of your fellow man and woman before material pleasures and you passed the test where others have been given the test and failed due to, still not understanding money and material gifts cannot help the soul's journey and its growth, "True Love" is only given unconditionally, and no amount of money or gifts given will ever give you the souls ability to Love and Forgive Unconditionally that must start from within.

We must all be prepared to put our own pleasures last if it means helping our fellow human beings first. That is what really is important and it seems in a world where the motivation centres on money and profit at the expense of our fellow brothers and sisters. Unless we get back to the basic simple fact that we should be caring for each other, then – and only then – can we truly start to address the problems that we are encountering today.

We moved out of our hospital house and got a house on the Ardbury Estate, 7 Jolly Way, the number 7 was supposed to be lucky, and for a while it seemed that way. I got a job at the YMCA. Karen was in the nursery and that allowed Mary to work as well. I had passed my driving test at the first attempt, got a small car, a Datsun 100A and things seemed fine but again problems arose.

Mary was homesick and disappeared back to Scotland, partly because she was homesick and partly because we were struggling to make ends meet. It was then I decided I would try and never put Mary through any financial worry again. I went for an interview for a salesman's job and surprise I got it. I was thrilled and wrote to Mary to tell her the job I was offered was in Cambridge but was told that as I was Scottish they would transfer me back up to Scotland.

Mary and I got back together. We bought a 28 ft luxury mobile home. The train of thought being we would stay in it until we got a council house. We would then move it to a holiday location so we could escape at weekends. That was the dream.

Nine months later the company went into receivership. Back to the drawing board I thought. The amazing thing about selling is that selling is selling the world over. The only thing that changes is the commodity, meaning the principles of selling are the same whether you are selling food, clothes or toys. I managed to get a job selling toys. My Manager John Crooks was to become a close friend over the years. As each company I joined seemed to go into receivership or was liquidated. I thought 'what must I do?'
I tried so very hard but all to no avail.
By now I was totally blind to everything that was happening round about me.

We managed to get a council house in Girdle Toll, Irvine; after my local MP David Lambie convinced Cunningham District Council we were not travelling people. The Girdle was a nice place. We were lucky, Jim and Mattie Wilson on one side, Sandy and Shirley Montgomery on the other side. Jim and Mattie although very private people, were amazingly warm people – always a nice friendly word for me when I lost a selling job, but were amazed with the different amount of cars I had with my job. Jim was immense with strength and stamina.
After finishing a long day with a landscape firm Jim still had time to help me pull my garden around and help me put up a greenhouse.

Everything in life was great a good job all be it quite erratic at times but I suppose that is the exciting part of the selling industry not knowing what is going to happen next.
Mary was developing asthma, yes, she always had asthma but not as noticeable. Mary took a real bad asthma attack and ended up in hospital, even then I was still too blind to see or was I scared and did not want to acknowledge what was happening around about me.? Whatever the reason I remained blind until one night I drove into my drive just as Jim was parking his van up for the night we would always talk for a short time before going in to get our dinner. There was something different about this night as I sensed there was something wrong and yet again, I did not understand this feeling within but nevertheless I said "Jim is everything ok?"
His eyes just filled with tears, you better come in Robert.
He asked me to take a seat as he had something to share with me.
He went on to tell me Mattie was in hospital... my own neighbour was in hospital and I never knew. Now that is real blind!

Jim explained that Mattie had collapsed twice and the local doctor said it was just all in her head. The third time she collapsed she was taken by ambulance to Crosshouse hospital, then transferred to the southern general hospital in Glasgow. and Jim was told she had been given one week to live.
I got up from my chair and went to the bathroom and cried like a baby. My neighbour Mattie that had been like a second mother to Mary and I and also there for our three children was not going to be there one week from today it seemed so final so cut and dry.
I thought this cannot be happening to two very special people! I composed myself and entered the living room and I asked Jim could I please go and see Mattie as I loved them both. Jim said yes but on one condition, I said anything Jim as long as I can get to see her. He said don't break down in front of her as she is unaware of how serious her condition is. I promised Jim and later on that night I went to see Mattie with Jim his three daughters and two sons in law were already there.

John one of the sons in law said “I have come out to let you in Robert” I leaned over gave Mattie a kiss and with a big smile said come on Mattie we all want you out of here so hurry up and get better. I sat holding her hand, she smiled squeezed my hand tightly as much to say you know I am not coming out of here! As I sat holding her hand, I became very conscious of the time that had passed and was thinking here am I depriving a family member of quality time with one special lady. So I arose and said I will let John and Kenny back in to see you, she griped my hand so tight and said I don't want you to go yet Robert. What could I say, the emotion that was I was struggling to keep in control but I promised Jim I would not breakdown in front of Mattie and I kept my promise to Jim. I left a little while later and that was the last time I saw Mattie alive. I can still today remember standing at the graveside one-week later tears pouring down my face thinking to myself how lucky all the family was to get to say goodbye in their own way. After all God blessed them with that opportunity which a lot of people sadly don't get the chance to do that. How many of you reading this wish you had that opportunity to say goodbye? I think in an instant I was given my first spiritual lesson and that is “nothing lasts forever”, That experience was to open my eyes slightly and make me realise that once we get caught up in the materialistic world we lose sight of what is really important.

Mary's illness was gradually getting worse. It was not helped by the fact that our son Mark, who has always been a sensitive wee boy, did encounter problems at school. Yes, he was no angel, but he was like any other wee boy, cheeky face, and unfortunately being caught and blamed for a lot of things that, frankly, were not his fault. But nevertheless, he was blamed for it anyway.
I went to the Headmaster to try and sort things out because if nothing else in life, I realised you must take responsibility for your children and you must be responsible in order that you bring your children up, not only in a loving stable environment, but as equally important, you must teach them right from wrong. That was not only a duty to your children but in broader terms that affects many people in so many different ways in terms of interpersonal relationships.

It may sound quite boring but if you can, please bear with me, I will explain to you what I mean. It relates to something I said earlier that for every action there is a reaction.

For example, a child who is left thinking that Mum and Dad don't love them will hit out and although it takes many forms, the child feels that they do not need to be responsible in the short term. You may think 'so what' but in the long run society suffers. That is born out today – we see nothing but greed in terms of profit crazy attitudes coming before people. We turn our backs on the homeless, the hungry. We do everything in our power to stifle the truth. Why?

You see my Mum always told me if you tell the truth Robert you will not always be liked but people would respect you. It is time that society woke up and realised that. Unless we take stock of the simple values in life, i.e. caring for each other, utilising God's resources; water and sun.
Since I was a little boy and being bombarded with images of deaths, starvation, famine from third world countries, I often thought to myself, in quiet moments, man can split the atom, he can walk in space, he can fly at the speed of sound! why can't he build a pipe that could take water to these third world countries that already have sun that is needed for the growth of crops, but lacks the rain?
Yes, it would cost a lot of money to finance this but you cannot tell me it could not be done because God has given us special people with the skills and knowledge. But man in his folly in this country wants to privatise the very thing that God has given us for our own very survival, which has already resulted in human suffering by being disconnected from the water supply.
If you follow that through with no water to flush toilets, bathing, disease will inevitably take its toll on human life once more.
So you see we do need to be more responsible. The truth is we are all interdependent on one another.

Enough of this, as I was saying, Mary's condition was worsening. Mark's teachers were complaining that he was disruptive, breaking pencils, so we decided to take Mark to a Child Psychologist as the Headmaster was saying he was becoming uncontrollable and was even threatening to expel Mark. We took Mark to the doctor and over the next three months an assessment of Mark was made. The report concluded Mark was a healthy normal boy.

I was to arrive home early from work to finish some important paperwork to find Mary sitting in tears. I asked "what's the matter?". The school had been on the phone, Mark had broken a pencil. Mary started to take an asthma attack and that was the only thing that stopped me from going straight to the school and to the Headmaster. Mark came in from school soaking. He said "Dad I am sorry; she would not let me go to the toilet". I said "that's it Mary, I am going up to sort this pompous guy out". She said "Robert, do not hit him". I said "Mary, my Mum always taught me the power of the tongue is always more powerful than the power of the fist".

I approached the Headmaster but his teacher could do no wrong. I then stated that if Mark should come home wet again, I would pursue it through Strathclyde Region. At that I was assured it would not happen again. I told Mary and she said "let's move Robert, that's the only way". I said "no we will stay here Mary. We have bought this house, we have done a lot to it in terms of improvements, in other words new double-glazed windows, central heating, new bathroom, shower cabinet, new fitted kitchen, pine panelling. Now we have got ourselves a very good home". But in the back of my mind I thought, what Mary wants she gets. It wasn't long after this that Mary took a bad asthma attack and was rushed to hospital. Mary said "all this worry Robert – let's move". I said "okay" but it would be nearer my Mum and Dad in Saltcoats. Mary said "right okay". I came in from work two days later to be informed Mary wanted to go and visit a couple of houses. The beauty about Mary, when she has set her mind on something it was achieved.

When she saw the property advertised, we went to see it in Stevenson, it was a bungalow near the station. It was nice but had landslide problems.

We also looked at two flats in Garven Road, the idea being we would knock the two into one and make it a very large living area. That also fell through. We were told by our Estate Agent that a property had come up in Saltcoats, which was ideal for our needs. It was in Braehead Place. For all that I was brought up in Saltcoats, I had never heard of it. Perhaps I should have gone with my gut feeling that it did not feel right.

Always pay attention to your feelings that is our way of giving you a warning to save you from pain and heartache if you will only listen to it you will save yourself a lot of pain.

Anyway, Mary had made an appointment for the following day. Just before we left to view the property Brian, a dear friend, arrived. Looking back I did not realise what a dear friend he would turn out to be. The three of us set off to Braehead Place. My first thoughts were, as we walked in through the back door, were 'oh my god, this needs a lot of work done on it'. And although I was a keen DIY man, the task before me seemed enormous. Mary was already in love with the property and nothing was going to persuade her otherwise. I asked Brian "what do you think?" He said a lot of work would be required but it could pay dividends in the years to come.

Thinking back to that conversation I thought 'you are right – years ahead'. Have you guessed right, yes, we moved in. It's funny how Estate Agents say offers closing at midday Friday and yet Mary was phoned at her work at 1130 am and told the property was ours.

I knew all along that it was going to be hard work but never imagined just how hard. It all started with Mary falling through the chipboard in the kitchen area and, on closer inspection, we found that they had not fitted a waste in the sink, resulting in two feet of water below the floor area. That had a knock-on effect of the electrics being out of action in the kitchen area. We had to rip apart the kitchen and have a new concrete floor area put in.
Of course, that also meant having the plumbing and electrics done also. I was not a very happy man but that's the exciting part of moving into an old property. You can refurbish it to your own taste. And the next problem was two plastered walls in the front room falling down. Very minor in comparison with what was about to unfold.

Karen and the two boys went to bed early one night. Mary and I had just sat down with a coffee enjoying the peace and quiet when Karen came downstairs to say water was pouring from her light bulb. In fact, it came from the roof area which needed repaired also. I went up to the loft area and sorted it out. I thought 'God what can possibly go wrong now'. I should have kept my big mouth shut.
Mary and I were lying in bed when Brian shouted, "I can see the town hall clock and I can see the time". I said "I know Brian from the bedroom window you have a good view". "But Dad, I can see the clock from the stairs". Mary and I jumped out of bed to see the plaster had fallen off on the outside and on the inside. The false wall had fallen in on the stairs. It was obvious, due to the amount of rain that had fallen; it was enough to bring down the lot. Well, little did I know that this was to be the start of events of the enormity that I even with my imagination could not have dreamed up. As the wall had fallen down it revealed a wooden beam which was not only saturated in water but had a fungus on it of enormous size.

Mary was developing chest infections but we never knew why until this fell down and realised that the reason was due to the spores. It was obvious the spores were affecting her. This was February 1990.

I came in one morning from night-shift as I had been working for a Stewarton bus company. One of the contracts was with Caledonian Express and I used to drive from Glasgow to Aberdeen. It meant stopping over, sleeping on the bus and returning first thing in the morning back to Glasgow. On this particular morning I arrived back home to find Mary was finding it hard to breathe so rather than go for a sleep I stayed with her. We decided after her breathing had returned to normal we would go for a special Chinese lunch. Mark had been kept off school so he came with us. After lunch we came home and Mary said “Robert please go for a sleep now that I am feeling better”. I said “okay” against my better judgement.

I was awakened abruptly by Karen my daughter saying “Dad, come quick, Mum can hardly breathe”. I jumped out of bed to find Mary sitting on the bath gasping for breath. I said “Mary hold on I will phone the doctor”. I ran through the room and phoned.

I helped Mary into the bedroom. The Doctor soon arrived, Dr Robertson. He gave Mary an injection which she did not respond to. I said “will I phone for an ambulance?” He did not respond. I said “will I phone for an ambulance?” The Doctor replied “yes”. I dialled 999 thinking Mary is only 34, everything will be all right. I explained to the controller that Mary's breathing was failing, the Doctor was in attendance and could they send someone as soon as possible. The controller was very reassuring. I said to the Doctor “I will nip downstairs and look for the ambulance coming”. I said “I will be up in a minute Mary; you are going to be okay”. I ran down the stairs and as no sign of the ambulance I thought I will nip back up and let Mary know everything would be okay.

I entered the room to find Dr Robertson trying to start Mary's heart. Her face was blue. He said “you had better phone the ambulance again”. I did so…

They kept trying to shock her heart. It took seven or eight attempts to start her heart but her lungs were not responding.

They ran out to the ambulance and brought in a mini ventilator. Mary slipped away twice after that but was brought back, and put on life support system. They worked on Mary for over three hours. I sat waiting thinking this is not what is supposed to be happening. Mary is stronger than me. I should be going first as Mary was very strong and I was very sensitive. I could not cope.
Mary came through her ordeal. I on the other hand was not coping. I couldn't eat, or sleep as every time I closed my eyes, I could see Mary's face laying there blue. Looking after the kids, working, it was such a struggle. Mary was back at home, I kept on thinking after all the redundancies and out of work we had experienced, we had moved here, a new house, a new job, everything should be great – it wasn't!

One day I came in from work. Brian my son had said something cheeky to me. I turned around and before I knew what was happening, I slapped him. I then packed a suitcase and was driving up to Stewarton with my uniform. I remember going in and ringing the bell and saying "here's your things, your uniform, I can't cope any more, goodbye". I jumped into my car and drove up the Glasgow road. I vaguely recall going into what appeared to be a rubbish tip and digging out of the dirt a yellow pipe.

It was really weird; I could see myself doing it but was not aware I was doing it. I washed it in a dirty puddle, put it in my car and drove up the road. I stopped at a field gate, drove through, closed the gate, drove through another gate and closed it. I then drove behind hedges where you could not see the car from the road. I got out, put the pipe in the exhaust and in through the window. I put a music cassette on, Elton John was the choice, a man that was so inspired by God through his music. Anyway, I spoke to God from my heart probably for the first time in my life. You see, prayer is fine but if it is said with no feeling or revealing the real you then it is just empty words.

Anyway, I settled down to die and simply said “God, forgive me I can no longer cope”. If I give you my life Mary will have to look after herself better. I love her so much and the kids need their Mum more than me so please take care of them all. I closed my eyes fully expecting to wake up in hell fire. The Catholic Church has a lot to answer for!! But God did hear my cry in the wilderness because soon after a man opened my door and said “you will not die, you have work to do here first and are a Christian man”. Me? I think not, but how does one measure a Christian? By going through the motions of going to Church or putting in a donation to someone who knocks on your door? No, I don't think so. I personally think it is more in the way we treat each other and our openness, our honesty, our forgiveness, our understanding – a genuine ability to forgive and not to judge.

You see, people only see the person they want to see because it suits their purpose. The examples are rampant in our Society today from mainstream churches who practice 'love they neighbour' but only if the contribution is there and they conform to what we tell them to do. They as the individual cannot express an opinion without the fear of being cast out of the group.
You see, as someone who was brought up in main stream Catholicism, I as a very young boy could not understand why someone could get drunk, beat up their wife, say three Hail Mary's, and all was forgiven until the next Saturday night came around again. I think what I am basically saying is you must take some responsibility for your own actions, although it has taken me many years to realise that fact and it was while I was in hospital I had time to collect my thoughts and analyse them deeply.

Mary was very angry that I had tried to commit suicide and did not want me back. Through all the madness of what happened I suppose I understood her feelings but did she really understand me? You know, the funny thing is Mary had a heart of solid gold. She dedicated her life to helping others, but did she really understand me?

In the spiritual dimensions there is no religion as this was a human made thing to keep people in line so they would never question the truth.
It was also to give the few money and power over the masses but as we have explained earlier money, power, ego, will not buy you a place in the spiritual dimensions.
That will be the first thing you All will Learn on returning to your original destination and you may have to return to learn but more importantly understand that the soul is here to learn that everyone that comes into contact with you is either to learn one or both of you a lesson and as your soul grows in compassion ,understanding ,love and forgiveness.
Then and only then it will complete its journey and then return many light years home. Back from what your understanding is the earth plain, but the truth is this is the testing illusion plain.

Never judge anyone you don't know what their journey is all about.

If I had told her I tried to take my own life so she could live and the children would have their Mother as they needed her more than me. I was the one who would tell them what to do, teach them what was right and what was wrong., I was the one that was responsible for the discipline in the home which in truth I did not like to do. My father only hit me a couple of times and in truth I deserved it. He was working night shift at the time and he was in his bed sleeping my brother and I were down at the bottom of the stairs, he twisted my arm up my back. I went mental grabbed him round the neck and pushed him against what I thought was the door but in fact was the side panel consisting of 6 panes of glass. His bottom went through one and he got such a fright he stood up and got himself stuck. Now I had forgotten that my dad was up in bed and dully burst out laughing so much. I went upstairs to go to the toilet just as I reached the top Dad came out his room and slapped me on the face for causing all the commotion, he hit me so hard it left the imprint of his hand on my face. I remember my Mum saying James (my dad) you hit him really hard as she had heard the smack from the kitchen below. Once I went to the toilet and washed my face still the mark was there and would remain for the next 2 to 3 days. Now before anyone thinks it was wrong to hit me I would say no. It was not as I learned a valuable lesson that morning as my Dad never had to hit me again, it taught me something that is really lacking in our society and that is respect. Yes at the time I hated him, but after some time I realised it was out of love I was being disciplined and yes learnt the lesson. Not only did it hurt, but I was also made to give up my pocket money for a number of weeks to repay the cost of the glass.

After coming out of hospital I was banished to my daughter's room where Mary had died in and my daughter moved in with her Mum. Again, a fine example of one of the basic fundamental laws, for every action there is a reaction. Anyway, as I lay in the room, isolated, I thought how I was ever going to make Mary understand that I did really love her. I was becoming more and more withdrawn as staying in the room all I could see was Mary laying there blue beside me.

Here is the second valuable spiritual lesson learned and given to me by

The Divine

Tell the truth always, people may not like you but they will respect you for being honest and truthful and yes if they then decide to leave you it saves you years of wondering what If I had said the truth?

What was to happen next took me by surprise…

Mary, seeing that I was becoming more and more withdrawn allowed me back into our room together and came in one day and said "we are going to join the Focus Centre". This was a centre that was financed by local government; the centre was offering a wide range of courses from Photography to Computer Studies. We both went to the open day and I joined photography group. Mary joined a computer course and a secretarial course. The course which I joined was about basic photography. It was led by a gentleman called Hugh Hume, a quiet unassuming man. I spoke to him about being frightened about joining a group. He quietly reassured me I would be alright and no pressure was involved.

Looking back on that conversation I now realise that Hugh must have had an experience with someone who had suffered a nervous breakdown. This course, in itself, was not pressured but the pressure was from within. How very complex! Life and individuals are. One day Mary came home to inform me she had bought three charity tickets for a clairvoyant evening; one for my Mum, one for Mary and one for me. I said I was not going as I did not believe in it and that they told you what you wanted to hear i.e. you are going to win the pools and live happily ever after!

Mary persisted about the three of us going. Reluctantly I went. We met my Mum at the hall. What was to happen that evening took me totally by surprise? One of the mediums came to my Mum. Her name was Sally Buxton. The other mediums name was Margaret Dreyer. Anyway, Sally started to tell her personal things, how; she was hurt on her shoulder by a bus, fact. But this was never publicised, i.e. local press. She said she had a piece of card holding her right wardrobe door shut. Again, this was another fact.
By this time I am listening and thinking how well she has managed to be lucky enough to come up with these pieces of information. I am still thinking how many more people could accept these two conditions. What was to happen next was not only unexplainable, but was so devastatingly accurate it had I gripped in fear.
Not fear that I was in danger but the realisation that this woman could not have possibly known the following. Sally told me and my Mum that a small lady came forward to thank her for what she had done in the past… and not to worry, she was alright. Sally said the lady died of a heart condition while you were abroad on holiday and Bobby represented you at the funeral. All the above was so very accurate then suddenly Sally turned to me and said "I want to give you a cabbage". The crowd started to laugh. Sally just looked up and said "this gentleman is not fat – he is very ill". silence ensued. You could have heard a pin drop. She went on to say there is a lot of love coming forward for me. She then told me of something that happened 30 years ago. Yes, it was about the wellingtons and the request for my Mum to buy them in the summertime. When she then told me that it was because a little dog in the corner house bit my heels, I just erupted in a flood of tears. Sally simply said "we are not here to upset anyone, there is a lot of love coming forward for you" and she left me. With hindsight I wish I had not broken down as it may have prepared me for what was to come. The relevance of the message at that point in my life was to try and make me see, understand that everything that happens does really happen for a reason and although I was very sensitive in truth I did not fully comprehend why!

Being loving and caring are not a sign of weakness. It is in fact the strength that opens your mind and more importantly your heart to truly understand another human being and love and forgive them unconditionally. We are all on a journey of lessons to be learned but more importantly have the compassion Not to judge.

Anyway, one year almost to the day, Mary landed on a life support system again, but I was a lot stronger this time round, although I was once again heartbroken. I took her three red roses to her bedside as I sat watching her on the support system I thought I am going to tell her to get better., I leaned across, kissed her on her cheek and said "Mary, I have brought you three red roses, that is one for every ten years we are going to have together. The kids love you, I love you and we are going on holiday in September. Please get better". Two days later Mary recovered. She held my hand and said "I heard you tell me about our years ahead and about the kids and our holiday". Soon after that Mary came home.

Although Mary was on life support she heard every word you said to her which goes to prove that there is a life beyond the human life we understand believe it is true and you will learn more.

September came around before we knew it and we were driving down to Wales to Butlin's, Pwllheli. This was to be our last holiday together.

Somehow, I knew this deep inside me but was hoping I was very wrong. Mary took a bad asthma attack at the camp. I ran to the Doctors Surgery on camp. There was a crowd. I just rushed in and said “please help, my wife is coming, she can hardly breathe, and she has been on a life support system twice already please help her”.

“It's okay, calm down” - as they rushed Mary into a side room. The Doctor came straight through, put Mary on a nebuliser and gave her an injection. She pulled through. My son, wee Brian, took a stomach infection and landed in the local Hospital overnight. A couple of days later he was back to himself. We were at Pwllheli for two weeks. Money was tight but I was determined Mary and the kids were going to have the best holiday ever. They were given money every day. Mark managed to turn what he had got into much more at the amusements. Mary and I slipped out of the camp three times. The first was to go into Pwllheli itself to see “The Silence of the Lambs”. To sit there in the pictures with my arm around Mary was like being taken back to the times we started going out with each other.

The second time was to Portmeirion, the village where The Prisoner with Patrick McGoohan was filmed. The peaceful feeling I got walking around the village I cannot describe. It was immense. If you get the chance, please go and experience it for yourself.

The third time was a half day coach tour up in the mountains. Not only have I got photographs of our holiday together, more importantly I have the memories which no-one can ever take away from me. We had taken the kids out for a trip to throw a pot and we all had a pot to take home with us our holiday ended too quickly for us all. Driving out of the camp all was quiet – the excitement gone. All of us had different thoughts, feelings, feelings of sadness, for the children their holiday over; for me the thought that this was going to be our last holiday together as a family.

Why? Oh why is life filled with so much pain God?

Because the soul is on a human journey to grow and learn and understand the lessons that will give it the enlightenment it needs to cope and deal within the spirit world where you will all understand on returning home to your natural home and existence, where you can and will freely move between all the spirit realms then and only then will you fully understand why!!

Love from all within the divine realms

Mary was still high as a kite; her own holiday was not over. The following weekend Mary was going to Amsterdam with the girls from the girdle toll keep fit group. I stayed at home watching the kids for the weekend and although it was only for the weekend, I missed Mary so much. Mary came back and was excited about the holiday. It was at that time I decided we must try and get away for a weekend together to Paris or Amsterdam. That unfortunately was never to happen.

During the next three weeks Mary was in Intensive Care twice. 17th November 1991, started as any normal Sunday morning, having breakfast, Mary studying her shorthand, the boys out playing with their friends. The afternoon arrived, dinner on a Sunday was ate early, about 3pm, then we used to sit down and watch Bulls Eye with Jim Bowen. We were very lucky living in Scotland, not only did we get Scottish television (STV) we also got Ulster television, which meant we got a double helping of Bulls Eye.

This particular day was like any other except I had an uneasy feeling. Mary and I had a small disagreement, a row you may say, of what and for what reason I can't even recall. I remember she would not come and watch bulls eye though. Karen and Mary had a row of which to this day I do not know what about.
Sunday evening I would always play darts with my Mum and Dad. Mary was always pleased about getting rid of me for an evening. Just another Sunday I thought.
I left my parents home at ten pm, came down the road to find Mary sitting relaxing, playing a computer game caller hyper action. I sat beside her on the floor, kissed her and said “I missed you Mary”. No response, just one of Mary's wry smiles. She said “you smell of smoke every time you come down from there. My asthma is playing me up I am going to bed”. Half an hour later I went to bed I kissed Mary and said “I love you”. I said that to her every night before going to sleep. It must have been about another half hour when I was aware Mary was having an asthma attack. I got out of bed, put the light on, got her peak flow monitor which measures her breath; it was failing so I said “I will phone for an ambulance”. Mary said “no, I will be alright”. I said “it is better to be safe Mary” and dialled 999

Mary got up and I brought her downstairs all of the time reassuring her I was with her and I would protect her. The ambulance arrived and we got her out and into it. The Doctor arrived and started to give her an injection and also a nebuliser inhaler.
I was holding Mary's hand – I suddenly felt Mary is not going to make it this time. I said “Mary I love you so very much, fight please fight”. Mary could not speak but with her thumb on my hand she moved it slowly three times. I took that to mean “I love you", I knew what she was saying.
Mary then became unconscious. I stepped out of the back of the ambulance which was still at my front door. One of my neighbours came out and gave me a cuddle. I just shook my head. I could not speak. I went back into the ambulance to be told they could not stabilise Mary.

They would take her to the hospital. I followed in my car behind watching the blue lights going round and round, driving down the bypass saying "God please let her be okay". Mary was rushed into resuscitation and I was taken into a side room. I had hardly settled in my seat when the Doctor came in and said "I am sorry, we did all we could". In those few words I died.
Mary, who had cared for me, loved me; made me feel safe, stood by me when I failed, was gone. This very special lady who I promised I would take care of and she would be fine, was gone. I was there to protect her. In truth, I couldn't. The family were called, Mary's parents and sisters were in Kilmarnock. Brian my dear friend arrived first as always and called them on my behalf. Listening to them saying once again we will be there for you Robert and the kids. That was a joke. After Mary had been on life support twice being in intensive care, me having a breakdown and them not appearing with the exception of Helen, the youngest of Mary's sisters. This is not me having a go at them, I loved each one of them and do so even till this day. I suppose looking back it was a human reaction to deflect the reality of what had happened!! Driving down the road I could think of nothing except how am I going to tell the children that their mother has died and I could do nothing to prevent it. I felt useless and helpless and all that was happening in my mind was shut out of the realities of life. As we were both unwell the insurance policy had lapsed. Yes, we tried to get it reinstated but once they found out Mary had technically died the second time on life support they would not renew it.
Our problems were only beginning.

Not only was there any money to pay off the house and money left over to bring the kids up on, there was not even enough money to buy food. I want to thank and acknowledge my sister in law Ann who went out to a butchers and bought meat and filled the fridge with food for the children and I. There was not even any money to pay for Mary's funeral as we were on state benefit. They would have to pay for it. The hurt I was feeling was compounded by the fact, not only could I not save the kids Mum; I could not provide a decent funeral. I must state, for the record, the department of social security were wonderful in the way they treated me at which was one of the most difficult circumstances I have ever had to face.

I must also pay tribute to my cousin Bill who provided the music and the order of service. I put the service together which included Mary's favourite songs, but also the children got to pick the Salvation Army's hymns as Mary was Salvation Army as were the children, young soldiers in it.
When faced with extreme difficulties it was heart- warming to find people who really cared for you.

The family gathered in my home and I said to them all that there was no money and that I would have to approach income support. Brian my trusted dear friend picked me up in his car and ran me everywhere, for the death certificate, to sort things out with the department of social security, down to the funeral directors. I could never repay Brian in money terms but the only way I could ever repay him is to be there for him in whatever way I can.

Something inside me was awakening that I could not understand. Looking back, I suppose it was meant to happen. What was this awakening? It was simple – I was after 35 years opening my eyes and, more importantly, my mind. The clarity I was seeing things in a different light was very startling in contrast to accepting everything I had been told and believed. It was as though I was being truly guided. I started to read books, specific books I was directed to.

Three weeks after my wife passed away I was standing in the kitchen when I was suddenly overtaken by the feeling I had to go to a clairvoyant evening up in Resource Centre. This meeting was to change my life completely. It was 9th December 1991. The two mediums were Margaret Dreyer and Sally Buxton. That evening was and still is so clear and so fresh in my memory. It started with Sally coming to me just before the interval. She said there is a yellow glow above and behind your head which has now changed into a gold wedding band.

Sally then said "have you just lost your wife sir?
Me: "yes three weeks ago"

Sally: "I have this lady here; she passed with a chest condition. She tells me you have three children, two boys and one girl and the girl has a mark on her left leg. She tells me you like special curry".
Me: "Yes it's my favourite Chinese dish".

Sally: "She keeps on repeating the name Robert, Robert, I must get to Robert – do you know this name?"

Me: "I am Robert". "She says you are to love again, she is repeating it, but wait she says you have made a pact not to love again".

I just erupted in a flood of tears.

The two mediums came up and put their arms around me at which point I could feel a heat so intense that only a furness fire could have produced. But with this came a calm that I have never experienced before. What the mediums or anyone else for that matter did not know after Mary passed away when I was alone with her I said

"Mary I love you so much, I am young, there will be women in my life but I will never love again."

How could this lady know these things?

I thought as I sat there thinking back to my first encounter with Mary, Mum and myself, thinking I wish I had not cried when Sally came forward with those wellington's.
Perhaps I would have been made aware of events to unfold but on reflection I suppose the beauty about life is you never know what is going to happen next – all part of the Divine's plan.

Yes, Robert it is all part of our plan for you all.

There are many things that the human mind cannot comprehend. This is why we, yes we as I am not a single god have and as you are now aware chosen you and the experiences You chose whilst in the spirit realm to return here and go through all the pain that an individual would not normally go through in one life time experience, but would go through many Lifetimes and over a period of many years where on the human plane would seem an eternity.
We will give you an example of what we mean!!

It would be like taking someone's hand going to a beach walking to the centre of it and asking that person to go back to the beginning and count every grain of sand and meet each other back in the middle. In human terms you may think it was impossible but each one of you have become trapped in the illusion you all call reality!! You have always looked upon yourself as being weak, being sensitive when in fact you possess the riches of the universe of being able to love and forgive unconditionally and looking for nothing in return from any other human being.

Just goes to show the faith we all believed that the many tests we have set you and yes they have been in human terms at times testing you to the very limit of your human existence.

This has shown us and the people's lives you have touched while here on one of the many plains of existence that being and feeling blessed with the very simple things that give so much pleasure not only to yourself.
But trust us you have passed this onto many souls that have touched your life that you will never fully understand till we call you back to take your rightful place and be amongst the unconditional love that you have shown to others.

The next piece of information was to baffle me completely.

Sally said "the lady is now saying beware of Christians in uniform that appear to be Christian but are not. Do you understand this?
Me "No I don't but I will write it down anyway".

Sally: "She is now putting a red ribbon and a yellow ribbon in front of you, do you understand that?"

Me: "No"

I was to understand it the following morning when I opened the blinds fully. In behind them in a basket was a red and yellow ribbon.
Sally: "You have not to blame yourself sir, you did all you could. She is leaving now but says you will love again" -
End of message, beginning of new life…

When I say 'beginning of new life', I don't mean I stopped loving my wife, I stopped missing her, no what I mean is when you realise death is not the end …but the beginning of a new experience. It does help the fear process, overcomes the fear of thinking you are alone. Yes you may have family around you but somewhere inside the brain is telling you how isolated you feel, how vulnerable you are. But once you have received a message if at that same time you feel a warmth start at the top of your head and work its way right down your body, then you have experienced a deep spiritual awakening, because as you leave you will also experience a calmness never in your life thinking such an experience in this lifetime is possible.

This was to prepare me for what was going to prove to be the most testing time in my life.

The 15th January 1992 things that have clearly stood out – this was a testimony I gave in the Salvation Army Hall in Irvine as Mary and the children were young soldiers in the Salvation Army. Anyway, I stood up and said the following…

Life is a school house of learning and when we understand that we know death is not the end but a continuation of learning could I help anybody who comes to me for help if I have not suffered or been in trouble myself? All experiences makes one grow, makes one strong, forms character and gives one courage to face the future. Nobody need ever despair because nobody is alone in this world. There are many paths to God.
Not one religion has the complete answer but each one has its own faith. It is that that bonds the entire Universe.

I am a great believer in destiny, as Mary once said “what is for you will not go by you”. Many in life never find their true-life path. Listen to your inner soul and let the Holy Spirit direct you to learning the truth as it is presented to you. It may make you enemies or lose friends, or people who have admired you suddenly lose their admiration for you because they do not like to hear the truth spoken. It offends simply because they do not like to look at and understand themselves or look at their inner self and the truth it reveals about each individual.

Is this my destiny, pathway? I have found out things about myself in the past weeks that I would have never faced in the past. I stand before God today and can say with a truthful and clear conscience he has directed me here through the guidance of the Holy Spirit. Because whatever any individual thinks of me I know through the goodness of the Holy Spirit that good triumphs over evil. It is with this, and the words of Captain Boyd that made my inner- self, inner- soul, lead me on this pathway to help others and comfort others in the future.

I was given a message through a medium – was I very wrong to do so? I think not. If I had received support from my family, my church, I would not have to have to turn to them. I must stress I contain, in no part of my body, any anger, any ill feeling towards anyone in life and certainly not my family i.e. my own Mum and Dad etc. and my spiritual family i.e. all of you here today.

The event that has turned tragedy, Mary's passing, into a pathway of new life happened on 9th December 1991.
I was told many things on this evening but one was to change my life completely.
I was told by the medium to beware of Christians in uniform that appear to be Christians but are not Christians. I was asked did I understand this, and I said “no I did not”. It must be said the person who said the message, Sally Buxton, did not know me or Mary and did not know we were adherents in the army. In fact there might be people here who did not even know that anyway. I was told to write it down. Some days later a member of the Salvation Army called out of the blue, followed by my own father.

The Member said “I heard you have been to a clairvoyant evening, you will rot in hell fire and damnation and never see Mary again, or Jesus again”.
Let me say quite categorically I bear no malice or anger to this person, then or even now. In fact, the Holy Spirit took a hold of this situation and he has not only given me the will to survive, but more importantly showed me the path that will help others in the future for no monetary gain.

Jesus never said “Come into my Temple with five pence, fifty pence or a £1 and I will give you help”. This medium was raising funds for the old and did not even ask for petrol expenses. Remember my brothers and sisters that in the Holy Bible written in 1 Corinthians, to some are given the gift of speaking in diverse tongues and to some are given the gift of healing.
After this evening I will not see any of you in this hall again but we will meet up in the future of this I am totally convinced. Whether it be in the street or if you come to my home, my door is always open to good and bad alike. The good have a bad side to them and the bad a good side to them, but I only see the good in people, but we will all link up anyway after our physical life is over. I am certain of this.

Consider the man who all his life has been taught that hell fire and eternal damnation is the portion of all who do not come up to the standards of perfection demanded. After death with difficulty of ridding themselves of such thoughts, causes them to go through much misery. He is continually tortured by the thought that he is being a fool although assured that such beliefs are untrue; until he manages to discard them he will be unable to settle down in the new life where there is so much to be seen and more importantly to be learned.

Acts II regarding the Holy Spirit. The Philanthropist during his lifetime has had one thought, one object in view – the helping of his fellow men – as the greatest opportunity of all. For now he is free to devote the whole of his time to helping and comforting those who require his services.

If he takes up the special work of helping those who have just passed over, he will find work for every minute of his astral life. Remember it is less than two weeks since you sat here bowed in grief not even knowing for certain that death was the logical sequence of life. Now at least you know something and soon you will be given the opportunity of knowing more.

You are thinking 'why do not more people know this? Perhaps they have not asked for knowledge or help as you have asked.

Perhaps they are quite satisfied with one of the many orthodox religions which tell them to have faith and to believe that everything sent is the will of God. All happenings are certainly the will of God but it is easier if we realise why such things are. It is easier if there is a logical answer to every question. Also, if it is made possible for each individual who takes the trouble to prove things for themselves thereby making the exceptions of statements made on a basis of faith unnecessary. Faith is always good but knowledge is better – you must have faith whilst acquiring knowledge and whatever happens you must never lose heart.

Never say you will not love again!!
It is this Love that we are all here
to share, unconditionally.

Soon after all this happened, I joined a development group in Irvine and was very surprised to find that I was beginning to receive messages, albeit very small but very accurate. I became friends with these two ladies, no I became acquaintances of Margaret Dreyer and Sally Buxton. I was to become friends soon after and from the bottom of my heart I must thank God because these two people were to prove a constant source of strength of spiritual love that I have never experienced from anyone except from my Mum and of course from my wife Mary.

About five months after Mary passed away, I was sitting one afternoon, late afternoon, having a cup of tea when the door was banged very hard. So I went to the door to find my father at the front door and he said "Robert you have to help me". I said "come in Dad and calm down". I made him a cup of tea. He explained to me that my Mum had been arrested. I looked at him in shock and dismay thinking how my Mum could be arrested. Anyway, it transpires that someone in the Post Office in Adams Avenue had said my mother stole £20 and in actual fact what really and truthfully happened was that when my Mother went outside the Post Office she had picked up a £20 note that was on the ground. The woman saw this and then accused her of stealing it. At this point my Mum had no opportunity whatsoever to either take it in to the Post Office or in fact get in contact with the police. The police were called and, as my father started to explain, they took her down to the police station and have charged her with theft of a £20 note.

Now this has all been documented by my solicitor and he will confirm this if asked. His name is Gordon Arnott Ghee and what a true angel God has put before me to help me through one of the toughest times again I had to face. My Father explained that she had been charged with theft and taken to the police station where she currently was being held. He did not know what to do.

I said "don't worry I will get in touch with my solicitor", who as I mentioned before was Gordon Arnott Ghee. I explained to Gordon what had happened and he said "Robert, when you have all the information, come in and see me tomorrow and we will sort this out for you".

Now, on reflection, at the time you really just don't take in the enormity of what is happening to you or in fact to your loved ones. My Father was distraught. He didn't know what to do because he was a very quiet man. My Mother when she came home wouldn't speak to anyone so I left it and went up to see her later on that evening. As she sat in bed I sat beside her and asked her what had happened and I simply said "Mum, if you have taken the money it wouldn't stop me loving you" and she looked at me and tears started to stream down her face. She said "Robert I never took the money, I picked it up and all of a sudden all these people were round about me accusing me of stealing £20. The police were called; they took me down to the station. They first of all searched me in the street," and as anyone will realise for a 62-year-old woman that is a very frightening experience. Nevertheless, they proceeded to go through her pockets and through her bag. They took her then into the police car and on the way down to the station picked up what appeared to be another £20 and said "we are charging you with the theft of £40".

Now it was originally only one £20 note and my Mum was in tears and distraught. Having gained this information I made an emergency appointment to speak with Gordon, my Solicitor, and the following morning Gordon informed me that one £20 doesn't suddenly turn up into two £20 notes and certainly not falling in the back of a police car. So anyway, Gordon said that he would proceed and subsequently asked if I wanted represented for this and I said "yes please". He then wrote to the police and the chief constable and as we awaited a reply, which seemed to go on forever, my Mum was becoming more and more withdrawn.

As I had stated earlier, Margaret Dreyer and Sally Buxton were very good friends and I accompanied them down to the Ryan Centre in Stranraer this one particular evening. It was an evening of clairvoyance and on the way down in the car both Margaret and Sally said to me "you are very quiet Robert, what's up?
And I said "nothing".

Anyway, later on, just prior to them going on stage, they asked me once again and I burst out crying and I said "my Mum has been accused of stealing £20 and I am waiting on the police coming back through my solicitor". Margaret Dreyer's words were at that point not to register but later were to register big time within my mind. She simply said "for a 62-year-old woman the shock of this is enough to kill her". I said "yes" not even realising what I had said. A few weeks later, my Mum was again withdrawn and I went up to see her two days prior to her passing. She appeared to be okay and I said "don't worry my solicitor has got all this in hand, you don't have to worry about a thing". She said "Thank you Robert your dad just doesn't know what to do" and I said "you don't need to thank me; I am here for you as you have been here for me all my life". Anyway, Saturday morning I am in bed when all of a sudden, I see a face appear before me. It was my Mum's face and she smiled, and then I saw this ship sinking and bodies floating everywhere. I thought 'that's really strange' then my Mother's face again suddenly appeared to me and smiled at me once again. She was just about to say something when the phone rang out and awakened me from my sleep. It was my dad. "Robert" he said "you had better come up, I have sent for the Doctor and the Police". I jumped out of bed and said "I will be right up dad".

I must state at this point I did not know what was happening, but as I drove up the road I thought my Mum was ill, telling myself she is not dead. I arrived, knocked on the door to be greeted by my Dad who just said to me simply "she is upstairs Robert". I ran up but I was too late. My mum was cold

I stood there looking at her telling myself 'this is a bad dream', it was not real. Sadly, it was and my main concern was to ensure my father was alright. I went downstairs and had a cup of tea. I sat there drinking my tea thinking Mary and I moved to Saltcoats to be near my Mum and Dad as my sister lived in Basingstoke and my brother was in Bury near Manchester. Mary's sisters were in Kilmarnock and I wanted to be near my Mum and Dad in case anything did go wrong. But I never imagined that within the space of six months Mary and my Mum would have passed away.

My dad asked me if I would organise the death certificate and go and identify my Mum as he could not face it. I said "of course Dad, don't worry". What was to happen next was most surprising. As I am writing this, I am fighting with myself.
Should I tell you the truth or ignore it? but because it is the truth, then it has to be shared. And hopefully once again will give someone who has experienced it and is frightened to share it with somebody thus them going through their life thinking it has only happened to them which leaves them once again without any answers!! I bear no ill feeling for what was to happen, another valuable lesson I have learned is to forgive.
It gives you such peace of mind.

Anyway, my Dad said "what am I going to do Robert about the funeral? I said "you are a catholic, talk to the priest".
Margaret Dreyer came to see me to offer me support. My Dad was talking to Margaret as I was making a cup of tea in the kitchen and before I knew it my Dad said "I want Margaret to conduct a simple service for my wee doll". That's what he used to call my Mum.
I said to my Dad at the time "are you sure Dad?" He said "yes".
My Dad spoke to the funeral director and told him what was happening. I personally never took anything to do with the funeral arrangements whatsoever and in fact the truth was I said "Dad, Mum and you are Roman Catholics and the rest of the family may react badly if you don't go through the church".
Margaret Dreyer left and the undertakers arrived. I went upstairs and took off my Mums wedding rings for my Dad. Once they had taken my Mum away. I said "Dad I will go and strip the bed and put the sheets in the wash" he looked at me and said "you don't have to bother Mum only put clean sheets on the bed two days ago. Clearly my Dad did not understand, so I said it's just to freshen up the room for her coming back. So off I went and removed the pillows and sheets for the washing. I brought them down and put them in the washing machine, after doing this I went back upstairs to open the windows. Then I went and also lifted the mattress and stood it on its end to freshen it up as well. When I turned round I saw two tablet bottles laying on the base of the bed. I picked them up and slumped to the floor, the thought ran through my mind.

Did my Mum take an overdose of tablets because she was so distraught about the police charges? and in an instant said to myself, Mum would not do that, she has never done anything wrong in her life. As I sat on the base of the bed clutching these bottles my mind in turmoil should I tell Dad or say nothing?
I was brought up by both my parents to always tell the truth and was told from an early age if you tell the truth people may not like you but they will respect you!
I went downstairs a short while later and made another cup of tea for Dad and I told him what I had found under the mattress. I will never forget the look on his face of fear and pain. I explained it may be nothing but, in my heart, I was saying to myself why put the bottles under the mattress?! It was at this point my father instructed me not to say anything to anyone. I was to go and identify Mum before they carried out the post mortem, I was then to obtain the death certificate and bring it to Dad without telling anyone how she passed or showing the family the death certificate. That was my Dads instructions and I would honour his wishes.

My sister arrived shortly after and all hell broke loose. My sister asked how Mum died and I said "I don't know I have to go and identify Mum before the post mortem and pick up the death certificate" I got a call from the hospital to say can you please come to Crosshouse Hospital to identify Mum before the post mortem was carried out. I was to attend at 2pm that day as I was driving up to Crosshouse praying and begging God that my thought was wrong that she had took these tablets. I arrived and as I was walking through the hospital, I meet a nurse coming off duty. She was the nurse that tried to save my wife months earlier in resuscitation and she said to me "hello Robert" I was taken aback that it had been six months ago and she remembered my name. I tried to smile as I shook her hand she said "are you here to visit" and I said "no I got a call from a secretary to identify my Mum before the post mortem" She just went chalk white and said "O my God Robert I am so sorry" then said they don't do post mortems here it is all carried out at Irvine central what time have you to be there? "just now" I said.

I must dash then as the appointment was in 5 minutes. I got to Irvine central as quick as I could but the person carrying out the post mortem had just left and was told I am so sorry you were sent to Crosshouse, but we will carry out identification tomorrow at 2pm. I left and returned home I was no sooner in the door and my Sister her husband and my Father arrived. She said "well what's happening" I said the post mortem was not carried out and was to take place the following day. "What did mum die of" she asked. My father just looked at me as if to say don't say anything Robert. I said I don't know but as soon as do I will let Dad know and he will tell you. She at that point went for me her husband grabbed me round the neck. As I pushed her away my Dad just stood there crying and saying "stop it Helen, my wee doll would not want this" My Daughter Karen was standing there and her face was chalk white with fear at that and as they left I was then accused of arranging the post mortem to suit myself. I did let my dad know what had happened with me being given the wrong information to attend Crosshouse instead of Irvine Central. he said "it's ok Robert do not let anyone know what is on the certificate, I will arrange to meet you and you can give me it then" I said fine Dad no problem. I went the following day to identify Mum and returned the following day to pick up the death certificate. I was so relieved to find that Mum had passed with a stroke condition and in truth deep down I Knew Mum would not have taken her own life. In all that was happening I never looked at the bottles to get the medication name off them and try to Google information. It transpires Mum had blood thinning tablets as she had problems with her arteries. Both Dad and I did not know a thing about her health condition as she had hid it from Dad to save him worrying about her.
I was then accused of involving Spiritualists in my Mum's funeral. Margaret Dreyer is a Spiritualist Minister but I did not involve her. It went from bad to worse. The Funeral Director whom I knew through him conducting my Wife's funeral literally a few months beforehand, phoned to say my Sister wanted me to attend viewing my Mum at a different time from them, meaning Helen, Alan her husband and my Dad.

Although you faced all of this on your own, we walked beside you at every stage and prevented you from another severe human breakdown. That is why in the church we filled you from head to foot in Unconditional Love to once again remind you that you are special and are part of the bigger plan of the vast dimensions you come from!!

As you and many others that are so Special and sensitive like you have suffered this treatment in the past and there will be a lot more to come. Again, this book will help all those that have suffered in the past and they will achieve great piece of mind. And those to come will also understand that those that inflict this type of emotional pain on others is in fact a truth that they are reflecting on the guilt they are feeling deep within and can't face up to the truth that revels them in their pure state.
Because Truth to them is one of the

hardest things for them to face up to while in the human frame, but face the truth they Must!! And when we take you back to the source of divine Love you will fully understand how important this book of teaching and wisdom is to everyone that is lead to pick this up

I can understand someone struck with grief and not being able to have clear thinking but my sister was very clear in her actions. I was then accused of arranging not only the post mortem but when the funeral was to take place as well. I was also not allowed in the family car that had been reserved for my Dad, Sister and her Husband Alan.

My Dad's Sisters were to come and vent their anger at me as well based on what my Sister told them. Between the three of them they emptied Mums house of her clothes and possessions; photos, ornaments, the lot. Having lost my wife after 16 years together and only six months previously before my Mum's passing I know you need time to slowly work through all the feelings and slowly as you gather strength you can then dispose of clothes to either cancer care shops or some other charity.

You do not wipe out overnight a person's existence. I could not understand what was happening but that was to be answered later.

My Mum passed away on 30th May 1992. One year later to be precise, 31st May 1993 I went to a psychic experience with James Byrne. I was to receive a message from my Mum and it said “let it go” … meaning the trouble with my Sister and then he said “Mary is here to say hello”. The lady who is with you, sitting next to you, is a good friend your Mother is saying”. So, as you can imagine I was very emotional so Margaret wrote down all the message for me. I decided from my first ever evening that I would write down not only the message but the date and time as well. One message I will never forget was given to me on 15th December 1991. It was short but was to prove very accurate… The message simply was the medium saw me in a vehicle and it was rolling but not to panic as it was not death. Sure enough some three months later March 29th 1992 a friend asked me to drive a vehicle from Kilwinning to Kilmarnock. I remember it was when the clocks went forward. Anyway, as you can probably have gathered, I rolled it in the process breaking a bone in my neck and extensive deep bruising on my legs where I had come up from my seat and hit the steering wheel.

The doctor at that time missed the broken bone in my neck as the x-ray never showed it properly. The Doctor said "it appears that the x-ray looks okay but I will get it reviewed by the consultant when he comes on duty later on in the week". He said to me also that the deep bruising had come from the bone outwards and I would be in a lot of pain for about ten days and was told just to take paracetamol to take the edge off the pain.

I came home and my daughter Karen met me at the door as I was ashen white and said "what's happened Dad?" I said I had been in a car accident. Anyway, as it transpires, I lay on the couch with my trousers off because anything touching my legs was very painful. When Karen, my daughter, saw the extent of the bruising she just looked at me and she went chalk white. I said "don't worry Karen; I am going to go to the church tonight and get a healing on my legs". I will be fine tripped of the tongue as I knew deep within, I was being protected.

Later that night I went along to the church which was fortunately just literally along the road from where I lived, and I received a healing. By the end of that healing session which only lasted literally five to ten minutes, I could feel the pain disappear and was ecstatic when I returned home walking as though I was a young child. Although the bruising would not disappear until ten days later, the pain had instantly disappeared.

Five days after this, I was driving along South Beach Road, that is in Ardrossan, and I saw my Cousin Jim standing in a bus stop and I thought as I drove past 'that can't be Jim, Jim passed away with a heart attack in the same year as my wife'. So, I did a quick U-turn went back, only to find it was my Cousin, his Brother, Alan.
I stopped the car and said to Alan "hi Alan, how are you? Where are you going?" He said "I am going to the cemetery to see my brother". I said "Well if you will allow me I will come as well as I was not made aware of the funeral and did not attend the funeral". I wanted to pay my last respects to Jim.

We sat in the car talking for a while at the bus stop and I said "I only heard two weeks after the event that Jim had passed away" and as we reached Princess Street in Ardrossan I said my wife had passed on the 18th November, two months after your brother. Alan said "no-one told us Bobby". I said "it's alright Alan, I know she survived death". I will never forget the way Alan just sat there looking at me. I said "I know it sounds crazy but you have known me most of my life Alan, you know I am not a liar, you also know Alan I would never hurt anyone and I would do anything for anyone in trouble if I could. I will explain what I mean Alan if you want me to". Alan said "carry on". By this time we were approaching Ardrossan Cemetery. We stopped outside. I said "I will show you what I am talking about". I explained about the December 15th message about me in a vehicle rolling and the Doctor saying I would be in pain for about ten days. I told Alan I went for a healing and I was no longer in pain. Now at this point Alan looked at me. I said "Alan I will show you what I mean with regard to the extent of the bruising on my legs". I pulled down my trousers and showed Alan my legs and the extent of the bruising. I started laughing and said "imagine sitting outside a cemetery showing your wee cousin your bruised legs, I bet you think I have flipped my lid"

Pulling up my trousers Alan said "thank God Bobby, I thought I was going mad and I could not talk to anyone".
"What do you mean Alan? I asked. "Well Bobby soon after Jim passed away I went to a workmates son's funeral. I was standing at that wall (pointing to a seven or eight-foot-high wall), I had my back to it, and I was standing alone when all of a sudden I felt Jim's hand on my shoulder. I have not spoken to anyone Bobby about this and what happened". The enormous strain on his face lifted and was replaced by contentment, this was in stark contrast to the way he was feeling only minutes prior.
Now at this point I knew why we met after all these years and knew instinctively from deep within me that truly there is a reason for everything that happens.

But you know you had not flipped your lid as we were directing you and people to you that needed help and answers

that is why we have placed you here in human form to help all those that need but more importantly want the help that the divine offers to all and gives through you

as you give of yourself your love and forgiveness to everyone you have ever come into contact with without ever looking for anything in return this is the true way of the divine spirit and you will return to the higher dimensions from where you came from.

God's plan, yes God's plan, is so subtle but very real that the answers are staring us all in the face. Let's stop this madness that has gripped each and every one of us, that lets us become so blind we spend most of the time wrapped up in ourselves that we forget a man, a human man, came to earth and taught us so many valuable lessons about love, compassion, understanding, forgiveness, putting others needs before our own.
Does it matter his name was Jesus, Harry or Gordon? No, in my humble opinion it does not. What does matter is we acknowledge our World is just that – Our World.

Fighting amongst the orthodox churches to what happened 2000 years ago is pointless. We should be more concerned with what is happening today. Church congregations are falling to the point that even the Church does recognise that it has a major problem.
Sex scandals affecting Church, Governments and Political figures it is little wonder that people lose faith when they are told sex outside marriage is a sin… but it's all right if you are a Priest, a Bishop, a Reverend, a Vicar or a Politician.

Whatever life has taught me, it has taught me this – you must tell the truth to first of all yourself, so you can identify with what you like and don't like about yourself. If you take the time to discover the truth about yourself and face up to it, God will always be beside you no matter what religion you are. In other words, take personal responsibility not only for yourself but for others around you.

The mainstream Churches and Governments for far too long have looked after themselves and not the people they should be helping! Anyway, I saw Alan once after that, a changed man was obvious. I have had many messages which I have written down but they are only meaningful to me and would serve no purpose to detail them as I think it would be more beneficial to reveal the real me, so at last my children Karen, Mark and Brian can understand why for years I have told them "I love you"

;

can understand the importance of forgiveness, understanding, and share with their own children some of the love Mary and I have shared with them. You know, at the age of 37, I can still hug and tell my father that I love him. Also my Brother and Sister but for them, the three of them actually find it difficult to open up and say "I love you too".

It is easy to say
I love you
But the real test of Love
is to forgive unconditionally.

It is important that you all understand yes it is difficult showing feelings and emotions because sometimes you may think people will think that you are soft, or weak but the reality is, if you express how you truly feel about another human being, that is the key that opens up the door for having peace of mind. Knowing full well that should one day you no longer see them, in other words they pass away, you will have told them everything while they were here. That will save many years of sitting thinking I wish I had only said this or only said that, by that simple action of saying "I love you" takes away many years of pain that you struggle to come to terms with.

I saw Alan one more time that was at my Mum's funeral. Sitting in the church singing one of my Mum's favourite hymns, on 4th June 1992, The Lord's My Shepherd. I again was being made to realise that death was not the end. I had a feeling of such immense warmth and love that helped me through a very traumatic time in my life. As I write this singing "Sweet Heart of Jesus" tears pouring down my face, I realise so many people need help, need love, need understanding.
It makes me realise how lucky I have been to have received all of the above and more.

*Luck has played no part in your life
you came here with unconditional love
and forgiveness in your heart
but more importantly within your soul
in your human form you will not understand
or comprehend this until you become
part of the divine once again.*

The next few months came and went. The children were not talking about their Mum, about their Grandma.
I didn't take the boys to My Mums funeral, I felt it was too soon after their Mum and I did not want to upset them. That was to prove to be a very big mistake Mark had been getting into a lot of trouble at school in and out of it.
I thought I was on top of it when, in truth, I wasn't. I was called into the school and was informed that he had better start behaving or a suspension would follow. Mark said he would behave, he didn't.

One evening his anger exploded. Mark said “I hate you, you are a bastard”. I just looked at him and my mouth dropped to the floor and said “what are you talking about?” Mark said “you didn't take me to granny's funeral and I never got a chance to say bye-bye”. Here is another valuable lesson for all in the future. Whether your children are young or not they deserve to know the truth. They deserve to feel part of the loss process and we as parents sometimes take the decisions for our children based on what we feel is right for them at the time. Sadly, children don't come with a manual and how to do things right or wrong. It is a learning growth stage for not only the child but for the parent as well. I for one have learned valuable lessons from that.

Anyway, we ended up at ten o'clock in the evening at Stevenson Cemetery where my Mum is buried, in the pouring rain. Both of us cuddling each other and I said to him “I am so sorry Mark,

I never meant to hurt you. I just wanted to protect you through the hurt of losing your Mum only six months previously”. As we both stood in the pouring rain cuddling each other, tears streaming down both our faces, I thought perhaps this is a healing process for Mark and hopefully the family would start pulling together.
It was not to be.

The following day I was called to the school to answer for his behaviour. I explained what had happened the evening before, explaining that would account for his recent behaviour. I was astounded to hear the Deputy Head say it did not concern him that Mark was missing his Gran; what did was his behaviour in school. I got up from my chair walked over to the desk he was sitting and quietly replied “it is obvious you have not suffered loss because if you did you would never have made that comment”.
I left straight after this knowing within my own mind the decision had in fact already been taken!

Mark was duly suspended, and had become distant, causing trouble, hurting the very ones that loved him, but it was not his fault, it was me that failed in respect that I could not take his pain away, nor Karen's, nor Brian's. I was trying to offer my support, my love; I couldn't reach any of them. That led me to feel totally inadequate. I tried to offer my Dad my love and support but I was really hurting inside knowing how bad they were all feeling.

I only hope one day they will understand me being an empath picked up and experienced all their pain individually and collectively and how proud I feel today even though I am no longer part of their life. I am so proud of each one of them as I know their young soul journey has been in human terms "immense" so I have nothing but total respect for each one of them.

The Lesson you were to learn in this
was that in human terms you cannot
take away another's pain from them
they must experience it for themselves as it
again strengthens the soul in preparation
for the souls return home
the miracles you have performed here
have gone without you acknowledging the
part you have played that is why you are
such a special soul and that is why most don't
understand when you say that You posses
nothing this is because your soul has no ego
just unconditional love.

Christmas came before we knew it. My dad went to my Sisters for Christmas and New Year. In truth, I was glad. I do not think in all honesty I could have coped. The New Year came, 1993, I thought please God let this be a better year. It was not to be. By the beginning of the year both boys were getting out of control, I kept telling myself that with love and time and understanding, things will get better.

In July my Gran died (my Mums Mother). I sat in the church thinking our family is disappearing fast. My Uncle Ron came over from Canada for his Mum's funeral and, because of the delay with flights, arrived at the cemetery just after we had laid her to rest. I asked him if he wanted to stay with me as he was staying for the week. He said “Tom's putting me up”. Tom being his brother and my Mother's brother. He stayed the week and went back to Canada. Three weeks later my Dad said, right out of the blue while we were playing snooker, “I think I will go over to Tom and May's for the weekend”. I said “that would be nice dad, it will be a nice break for you plus Tom and May will be delighted to see you”.

My father phoned on Friday 13th August to confirm it would be alright to visit, and off he went for the weekend. On the Saturday, 14th August, a medium friend popped in to see how I was getting on and over a coffee we sat chatting generally about everything and anything when suddenly she said "God bless you". I said "What is it?" "They have just rung bells in my ears". I said "What does that mean?" Phyllis said "it means a death in two days- time". I said "What? In my family, she replied "I don't know". But I knew she did know. Anyway, I dismissed it from my mind. Sunday came and went. Monday morning came. I again was sleeping when the phone rang out. I awoke startled and still half asleep, my Father was at the other end crying. "What's up dad?" "Tom is dead". Now my father has a brother Tom and I thought he meant him as he went through a very big operation just a couple of weeks beforehand but no, this was 'big Tam' my Mum's brother. Now I was stunned! If you said to me pick someone for a poster that depicts good health I would immediately pick Tom.

After I drew myself together, I said "Dad, I will be over right away". At the time I never really put two and two together, in other words the message on the Saturday 14th and getting the phone call two days later. The reason I give the dates and can be so very accurate, I write everything down as you can always check it and refer back to it. Anyway, I arrived at Tom and May's House in Dalry shortly after the call. May was in deep shock. She said "Come up Bobby and I will let you see him". I went upstairs with May. She explained on the way up that he had took ill and fell out of bed and it was a blessing Jim was here, Jim being my Dad. "His eyes rolled Bobby and he was gone". Anyway, at that she started crying and saying "What am I going to do Bobby?"
I held her in my arms and simply said "It's alright May, God will give you the strength. You have people round about you that love you and care for you and with their support you will get by, but your life from this moment on will change completely and never be the same" Which was exactly what I said to my Father while drinking tea that morning my Mum had passed away.

I spent a few minutes with Tom looking at the same healthy man that was only, in my brain, laying sleeping. It was like a dream but sadly it was no dream. May kept saying "If it was not for Jim being here I do not know what I would have done" To everyone coming into the house, my Dad said to me later "It's funny I picked that weekend to go to Tom's and I just thought out of the blue about going to Tom and May's. I said "God works in mysterious ways Dad", knowing full well that the chain of events, messages etc., are in fact Gods subtle plan and there is truly a reason for everything that happens to you on Earth and you must treat it like being back at school i.e. lessons to be learned…

The difference between school and life!
In school you are given a Lesson then a test
In Life you are given a test which teaches you a lesson.

I went to see May a few weeks after the funeral.
She said a lot that night and still clearly hurting, but one statement she made will remain in my memory forever and it was as if a valuable lesson was learned by her. She simply said
"Bobby I will try and change the way I have been to others in the past, you never know when God will call you and I don't want to go back to the Spirit world from this world with bitterness in my soul".

I was choking back the emotion that was running through my entire body thinking 'why does it take something like the death of a loved one to learn the lessons each individual has to learn?'.

When we take a soul home it is not to punish that soul or their human loved ones

It is because that soul has learned all the lessons that this journey was to teach them.

This has the effect on the human soul that is left here to re-awaken them. To look closely at why they are here in human form
and for some yes they do learn and for others they say I have learned a lesson I will change the way I feel and act towards others
then sadly after such a short period fall straight back into the Illusion of the material world. While others cannot cope and turn to other forms of getting them through their very long days.
What every human forgets is that you come into this life alone and go out alone, but become part of the one again. For some in the spirit world they are tormented by the feeling it is an illusion but in time with help they quickly settle down to which is their natural home and from the dimension they came from.

Sunday 21st August 1994 again started just like any other, but again this was to be another major event in my life that at the time I could not figure out as hard as I tried.
It started Sunday night at a local Spiritualist Church in Saltcoats. A lady I had never met before, a visiting Glasgow medium came to me. The message was as follows: The name of Mary had been called in (my wife's name), also Joe (My Guide's name). A Navy gentleman with me (my Dad's brother), I have been hit for five (the following passing's of Jim my cousin in 1991, Mary my wife in 1991, my mum in 1992 and my Gran in 1993 and Uncle Tom in 1993 as well, making up the five. I have to look forward to the future, changes ahead, seeing something to do with property in the future – not the right time just now – car will be easier money wise. Joe is saying "someone in the family is not pulling their weight" and Joe will be giving them a good shake remember what I have just said to you! She was correct, about the family not pulling their weight together. The two boys were constantly getting into trouble at school, giving cheek to people outside and giving cheek to Karen and myself. They were fighting between themselves. I was becoming demoralised and very near being broken. We all had lost the art of communicating with each other. On reflection, the main strength I had was in fact communication. How I felt I would always be able to tell the children "if you have a problem come to me and I will help you if I can, or "if you just want a cuddle I am here for you". Looking back, I am probably to blame. I should have made them aware of the house and why it was up for sale. I should have taken the boys to my Mum's funeral so that they could say goodbye but please Karen, Mark and Brian, believe me when I say I only wanted to protect you from all the worry, all the pain. How could I tell you that I promised your Mum she would be alright and I would protect her the night she passed away? I promised also I would take care of you and in reality all I have done is tried so very hard to fulfil both roles of Mum and Dad, but I can't provide the Mother role. Yes, I can cook, I can do the washing, I can bake, I can do the housework but I cannot replace that one very special ingredient which makes up

your Mum. Yes, I tried to take my own life but it was not through selfishness, it was because I loved your

Mum so much and you Karen, Mark and Brian that I decided if I took my own life your Mother would still be alive today to look after you as you really needed her more than me. I need the three of you to understand but more importantly learn this lesson.
I have only tried my best for the three of you. And yes, you can say I failed to protect your Mum. Yes, you can say the house was lost because I could not work through mental health conditions. Yes you can say I tried to take my own life and at the time probably never understood it but it was not because I did not love the three of you, in fact it was because I Loved you All so Much I thought by giving God my Life you would all be happy. I knew how much you all loved Mum and needed her so much more than you all needed me. But now I am sharing this, not in any way, shape or form to shame you or hurt you. The reason I am sharing all this information is for other families that are experiencing what we went through at least to have the lessons there for them that they can work on in terms of communicating better. Understanding that yes, each one of you has to go through that pain barrier on your own. I am not God. I cannot take your pain away as much as I wanted to, I could not take my Dad's pain away when my Mum passed away. I could not work because I could not concentrate and my mental health state was not good and as this book is now being processed in 2015 going into 2016 there are days I still struggle with some of the things that have happened and wonder how it ever got that bad. But, being a medium, and being an empath, has taught me that everything happens for a reason and although you may, or in fact you may not, have regrets for what has been said and done in the past, makes no difference to me because I love you all and that will never change. And yes I forgive each and every one of you, Karen, Mark and Brian, and all those within my own family that could have communicated better and been there for me instead of adding to my pain. But the reality in life is I am also human and I hurt as well but I do love and forgive unconditionally. So if you are now reading this book it means perhaps I am not here

but I hope in that reading this book you understand the man behind the man you saw as your father and some of the decisions that I

had to take. Not because I was a smart-ass, not because I was God, not because I thought I knew better, but because I thought I was doing the right thing for each one of you. There are many days weeks and months I still ask myself the question could I, would I have done anything different in bringing you all up the way I have. And on hindsight maybe I would not have smacked you or smacked the boys with the belt as I was when younger but here is the truth!! Although I smacked each one of you it was not every day as you all seem to perceive. Nor did I ever leave any bruises or marks on anyone of you and that is the truth!

I know perhaps you are not at a stage of understanding as yet on what we all went through, but as you hopefully read this you will have a greater understanding and see the bigger picture that all we needed was support from the social work. And not to rush the two boys into care and yes I still have all the paper work that proves there was not one bit of bruising. As I received the medical report when the boys were taken into care and that was further reinforced when Mark admitted to pulling his two teeth out and Brian confirmed that he has saw Mark do it.
Yes, I am sorry I shouted at you for looking at me and asking me if I punched his teeth out! But this is not an excuse nor is it in any way said to make you feel bad or upset you. But the truth is I was at breaking point with everything that was happening around at that time
Perhaps I was never meant to be a father to you all or even my two step children. But as the divine has made me aware I have done the job I was sent here to do and that is by going through all of this hurt and trauma.
This book will help so many others to realise that although your children come from you they are all growing souls sent to learn and experience the painful lessons that each one of us has to learn in order to grow. Yes, it is a parent's responsibility to instil values, morals, love, compassion, forgiveness, and empathy to others and to try and see the other persons view without judging them because they may be different to what we perceive they should be.

Each one is on their own souls journey and no two are the same.
And the reason for this is to learn everyone never to judge another soul on their journey as they will come into your life and for a short time or longer time.
Will walk on the same path way as you, each one giving you more understanding about the huge complexity that the Human faces on its soul journey.

Each one is a soul on a human journey to expand the soul's progression of understanding!

That is why it is only the soul that returns to the divine and Not the human frame.

As each returning soul brings with it more and greater understanding of pure unconditional Love and forgiveness. When you master this there is no need for returning in human form ever again

"This is a Truth".

I was sent here with unconditional love and forgiveness and yes I will return the same way, thus completing my journey. Yes, I know I will return to the spirit world without seeing you all again or the grandchildren that I have never meet, but again please don't feel bad about this. As I know this is one of the lessons you have to learn and more importantly understand that we do not own our children as they will make up their own minds.
I have been approached by your Daughter and Marks wife which both have said they have heard bad and good things about me, but would like to meet me to make up their own mind. As the two of you are aware both situations were thwarted at the last minute. But again, what you both probably do not know is the two of them apologized to me and my reply was I do not want you doing anything that would upset you. or My Children, again it is that understanding of unconditional love and forgiveness, although did hurt me the human, but my soul knew there was a reason behind it and lessons to be learnt either by them or both of you, in the bigger picture it does not alter the love that burns in my heart and soul for you all.
I am so very proud of you All because of all our experiences together in this short life. Many others will get to see and have a greater understanding and hopefully learn that there truly is a reason for everything that happens to you. The Divine is not punishing you or anyone for that matter, he has given each one of us the divine unconditional Love of free will to make our own mistakes, so we can learn and enrich the soul while here on earth. It is up to each one to learn and grow from the mistakes that we make often but never understand why it keeps happening. This book will give you a solid foundation to get the most out of your short life here.

After reading this and hopefully many will find the peace of mind like I have with the Divine giving these answers, know you All have made a real difference to many others in many different ways, from the answers from the divine that will undoubtedly change many others who are still searching for these answers and have been for many years.

Remember
while you are in human form there is no greater Lesson to be learned
but more importantly understood that making mistakes is the key to a greater understanding and if you learn from that experience your Soul will grow to truly understand unconditional Love and Forgiveness and look and see others so differently
that you no longer are in competition with one another and those with ego have been here many times before to learn the lesson that every soul is no greater or lesser than another soul
then and only then does the real soul emerge.
Life is very simple!!
It is people that are complicated.

One Tuesday night I came home from my meeting to find Karen very distressed. The boys had been fighting and called her names. I went in and told them that I had had enough and we should be pulling together instead of all this fighting. I went back downstairs to watch television; Karen came down and was sitting watching it with me when screaming and swearing came from the boys' room. I ran upstairs to find Mark sitting on top of Brian, choking him. I pulled Mark off Brian and I smacked Mark roaring at the top of my voice for both to start behaving themselves as I was feeling in need of support.

Looking back, it was probably very selfish of me to expect a 15-year-old, a 13-year-old and a 12-year-old to give me support. I was trying to support my children, trying to support my Dad, trying to help other people that were directed to me. We had reached a crisis point and I could no longer find any answers to the problem or see a solution. A few months previously I had received a message from a medium saying simply that Joe, (Joe was my Guide), would be giving the boys a great big shake up.

Now as you know, and I have said previously, I write all my messages down. It quickly went out of my head completely. Shortly after this message Joe appeared on the wall in Braehead Place and was seen not only by myself but by Jill from Dreghorn who was a fellow medium from the Dreghorn and Irvine church, also my daughter Karen.
Now I do not play with people's minds or their emotions, and I kept looking at the wall thinking I was again going mad because I could see his face clearly on the wall and it was as real as though he was standing right in front of me. So, I never said anything and both Karen and Jill said "Oh you see the man do you?" And I just could not believe that they could also see Joe.
Coming back to the solution of how do I rectify this was to be taken out of my hands and again it was Divine Intervention. I had been made aware of this but as you can well imagine, experiencing everything that was going on around about the time I found it difficult to concentrate and make any sense of anything in life at that point.

Coming back to what happened next. As I said Karen and I were sitting watching television and I heard all this commotion upstairs. As I said I quickly ran up the stairs and caught Mark sitting on top of and trying to choke his brother Brian. I had separated them and shouted like I have never shouted before and, on reflection maybe that was the end of my tether reached. However, I got them settled down and went back downstairs. Karen and I were sitting watching television when suddenly the door was pushed open and there stood Mark screaming and shouting at me saying I had punched one of his teeth out. I said "Mark, if I had punched you in the mouth there would be more than one tooth out, get to your bed". Karen looked at me as much to say "did you dad?" I said to Karen no I did not punch his tooth out Karen," shouting at her in the process. Karen stormed up to her room and the door was duly slammed shut.

The following morning, Wednesday August 23rd, all hell broke loose with the three of them fighting. I shouted at them like I have never shouted before. The effect was that the three of them were in tears. Mark said "I can't go to school Dad I have been suspended". I said "I don't care Mark you are going". I had not received any word of the suspension from school. I had to take out a group of ramblers for the day. This was a bus I drove for as a volunteer the last Wednesday of every month. I came home later to find a note from the local Police laying behind the door. 'Please contact us as soon as possible' my first thought was Please God Don't let anything happen to my Dad.

I went down to the Police Station and what happened next was to leave me confused, heartbroken and shocked. The policeman said "Mr Gallacher we are charging you with serious assault and breach of the peace, anything you say will be used against you".
At this point I expected Jeremy Beadle to jump out …but this was no laughing matter. He was serious. He explained that my son said that I had punched his tooth out. Karen went along with it because of the commotion she heard the night before and the breach of the peace was because I shouted at the top of my voice at the three of them. I told the policeman I never punched his tooth out.

Yes, I did smack him but no more than any loving parent and I said this will all come out in the wash, meaning that my Mum told me "Always be honest and tell the truth Robert! People may not like you but they will respect you" The truth always will come out in the end. The policeman then said, "I understand you have lost five members of your family and you have had a nervous breakdown. Your daughter Karen is concerned that you have been shouting rather a lot lately and feels you will have another breakdown. My advice, off the record (the policeman said to me) is to say you have suffered a breakdown. Go to the Doctor, tell him you are under great stress and could you go into hospital for a few days. This will help your case when it comes to Court" I was sick to the pit of my stomach., If I had done what he said they would go easy on you in court. "No" I said, "what you are asking is for me to admit I punched my sons tooth out and I am on the verge of another breakdown and hide behind this lie. No way! – I am innocent and I will prove it". But there was worse to come.

The children had been taken into care by the social work and they had taken a care order out on them. My world collapsed.

What the children did not know is my very survival was based round about them. Again, I have learned some immense lessons from this which will become apparent as you read on. I phoned my friend Margaret Dreyer as soon as I left the police station. She arrived shortly after at my house. I explained what had happened. She said "Did you punch him Robert?" I was hurt to my core that she even asked me the question; I said "No I did not". I went into more detail about the trouble the boys were getting into and how Karen's behaviour was getting worse, rebelling, answering me back etc. I said "I am doing the best I can Margaret. I take the boys swimming. Karen gets away on courses as she was in the cadets and she always gets spending money"

What I never realised through all of this pain and rejection from my own family was not about money or the lack of it.

It was the effect of their Mum not being there. Margaret went to see the children and came back and reassured me they were okay. I felt totally gutted and thought what is the point in this struggling.

The children don't want me, what's the point in living anymore?'

The point was I was to clear my name. I was to face the challenge put before me. I was going to fight back. You see, I thought God has brought me this far, he has not brought me this far to fail. As I have said before, I knew it would eventually come out in the wash and it did. The boys admitted they were lying but the wheels of the social workers were in motion and nobody was going to stop them. Basic errors were being made.
The fact there was no bruising; two teeth knocked out but in different sides of the mouth did not deter the police, social work or the school. Mark admitted to pulling not one but both his teeth out and Brian admitted seeing Mark pulling them out. But this was not good enough for the social work department. They were remanded in care. Now I had a real fight to get them back.
Karen was at the age where the social work department could not take her into care and she duly announced that she was going to live with Margaret Dreyer in Beith. This was a real blow to me but Margaret said "it will only be for a few days Robert". But as Karen was upstairs packing her stuff, I knew deep inside she was not coming back and I said this to Margaret. You know, deep inside Margaret was a stranger to her but it was most surprising that Karen never even considered Mary's Mum or Mary's sisters.
To me it was a reaction to all the times they were not here for her, but I was here for her. I could not understand why she did not want to stay.

You know, for me this is of great benefit to write all of these events down because it makes sense when events are detailed. It helps you to build up a picture that not only makes sense but, more importantly, lessons are learned and more easily understood.

So the lessens you have learned
and hopefully anyone reading this will learn
that when going to a church service if you are
lucky and blessed by the Divine to receive a
message Always write it down and date it and
put the time on it as well as this is the only way
you can verify the information given as it may
not happen on that day but in fact may hold the
first part of the jigsaw puzzle to your awakening
and understanding
that we walk your journey with each one of you.
We the divine always make you aware before of a
major event in your life
we put all the clues there for each one of you
and if now you understand that you All must
raise your awareness this will have a great
impact on the earth plain failure to do so will
result in many years of Why !! .

Visiting the boys in the early days was heart breaking. People looking at you and making up their own mind but only based on what they knew which was only their interpretation. There were snide comments and innuendos made that frankly were for me difficult to comprehend. I am not perfect and I know that. Yes I did shout at them and yes on occasions I did smack the boys with a belt which I had received in my childhood and it did not do me any harm, but, I never ever bruised them or hurt them so hard that they would have needed medical attention. Yes, I did stop their pocket money, yes, I did ground them when they were really bad but you have a duty and a responsibility to teach them right from wrong.

What the social work failed to understand – this was not about me hammering the children and being abusive to them. On the contrary, every single day of their lives they were sat on my knee, hugged, kissed and told that I loved them. This was about the family being in total crisis and needing help, not needing separation.

Mark and Brian, who I visited in the home, suddenly informed me that they were getting more money than I could give them and, in reflection, I look back on this now and think to myself I was giving Mark and Brian £2 pocket money each week plus they would get swimming two or three nights a week. But in the home Mark got £4.90 and Brian got £4. It went on age. They were treated to clothes costing £60 to £70 at a time. They got trainers at £50 a pair. I thought I could not compete on income support.
What I had to offer them was love, understanding and being there for them but again, in a materialistic world, it would appear it counts for very little even in your own family.

This was a very difficult period for me, not only having lost my Wife and my Mum, but also my children. Yes, I told them I loved them but in truth did they love me? Or was it just when the good times were there! You see another valuable lesson I learned through all the difficult times was Mary and I had was true love. This is only ever experienced through sharing good and bad times.

Two social workers came to my house. They sat at my table and my inner spirit told me one was laid back and looked at all the facts and decided what was best. The other one in contrast was extremely dangerous and would for her personal gain do anything to secure that magic word 'promotion'. These character reviews were given to me by Spirit thus enabling me to tread very carefully in both what I said and what action I was going to take.

Just before going to court, God intervened. A new social worker was appointed to my case and the two others were taken off it. As social work and the reporter did not have a case against me, I assumed they would drop the charges. Wrong! They were going ahead despite knowing the boys lied and admitted it. Despite me telling the social work to check the school records at Argyle Primary and speak to the head teacher who I had to go and see on many occasions regarding Mark making up stories. They never did! What they did not realise was that I spoke to the Head Master at Argyle Primary and explained everything that happened and I asked if he would attend Court on my behalf as a character witness. He agreed. The following day at court my friend Brian was there to support me once again. At the Court on the 11th hour the reporter wanted to make a deal. I was not interested. I wanted to go before the Judge and not only clear my name but get my boys back. All the police charges against me were dropped and the Judge's order was that both boys be returned on a 44/1-A home supervision order. It was then referred to a panel to put the final stamp on what the Sheriff ordered, but yet another gremlin in the works. At the Panel it was suggested that Brian be returned home and Mark remain in care for more work to be carried out with his school attitude. I protested and made it clear that I loved both my boys equally and wanted both boys home. Nevertheless, the decision stood. I will never forget picking Brian up at the home, Brian crying, Mark crying, me crying. I held Mark in my arms and told him I loved him and it would not be long before he was home. Driving away, Brian sitting crying, me looking in the mirror catching a glimpse of Mark standing at the window crying was a haunting sight which will never ever leave me. And in fact the home they were both in when this happened was on the Kilwinning Road in Irvine and although the home is closed, I try and not drive

past it as I can still see Mark standing in the window crying and although I have received many messages from not only my Wife but also my Mum and Mary's Dad Andy that I did everything I could to keep them all together and I have not to blame myself. Even to this day although the facts detailed here are accurate and is the truth and can be backed up by paper work I still have to this day and my solicitor can also confirm the details, I still feel I have let them down. Yes, my Spirit knows I did what I felt was right for them and from a spiritual point of view I also know I don't know what their Journey here is all about, but God knows I Love the three of them more than life itself. At this point in time I still don't understand Gods reason for everything that has happened.
I have never questioned the Divine or blamed him for anything. What I do know is I have paid a very high price for what I have thought was the right thing to do for them and No I am not looking for any sympathy what so ever as they also have suffered and came through a lot as individuals, and I for one are proud of each one of them.

Do not Judge anyone! Because you don't know what that person's journey is about. And in a breathe your life and journey can change forever, learn the lesson, love the person and move on with your own journey and yes sometimes that means having to leave your own family behind in order for both of you to learn the lesson and although it may be painful know when you arrive back home they will not be strangers to each of you as the lessons will have been instantly understood.

Brian was uneasy with leaving his brother, albeit they fought like cat and dog. Mark was back on a home visit when again trouble flared. I had lost all control. He just wouldn't listen to me. It was as though I just did not exist. Mark would wind Brian up about how much stuff he was getting, how much pocket money he was getting. It was not helped by the fact that Brian was told he was going to receive £60 to spend on his birthday but would only receive this £60 if he was back in care. Brian wanted a Sega master system 2 which he would have got if he had not been discharged. And He would have to go back into care to receive the money and obviously the Sega master system that he so desperately wanted, that I could not give him. One night when Mark was on a stop-over again trouble broke out and I sent them to their rooms. It then became very quiet and I thought to myself 'maybe they are just very tired and they have gone to sleep. I should have known that something was being planned, but I honestly thought they were just obviously very tired and had in actual fact fallen asleep. So I settled down with a cup of tea and was watching the snooker on television. Sometime later the front door was chapped and there standing at my front door was two workers from the home. In my naivety I thought they were passing and were popping in for a coffee and a chat. But no, the reason for their visit was that Mark and Brian had phoned them. I said "They can't have as I am on incoming calls only". They said "Mr Gallacher, you don't understand, they phoned from the station and told us you had locked them in their room." I said James don't be daft they are up in bed sleeping. Please come with me and I will show there is no locks on the boys room or in fact any apart from a bolt lock on the bathroom door. As we went upstairs, I noticed the velux window was wide open but never thought about it at the time. I said as I opened the door "look they are sleeping" only to find the room empty! What had in fact happened they went from the upstairs velux window, over the roof and down onto the outhouse. "They said you were shouting, hitting them and locked them in their rooms". Obviously the boys never thought they would check. I said "What is happening here James?

” He said “They have dreamt up all of this for their own ends”. I said “If I tell them off am I to expect this all the time?”

He said, “Come over to the home Mr Gallacher and I will read the riot act and tell them the lies must stop and they must show respect and do what they are told when at home”.

We arrived. James did read the riot act but undid everything on this following phrase - he simply said “If your Dad lays one finger on you or shouts at you, I will have you both back in care”. After that statement I was frightened to even tell them off.

What is happening in our society today is undoubtedly the result of punishment not being carried out? The withdrawal of the belt in schools was the start of discipline falling apart.

Brian ended back in voluntary care again because his attitude for his age was unbelievable. He would swear at me, getting into trouble at school. Deep down I knew this is anger coming out through the loss of his Mum. I feel desperately inadequate that I cannot help him with his pain, his frustration, his anger. The last straw came for me when I went to see him. He spat all over me. I felt totally humiliated. By this time the boys had been separated into two different homes because they could not cope with the two boys together. I know that logic tells me that if they can't cope, and after all they are the professionals, then I should not feel so inadequate and so guilty that I failed. But did I fail or did God intervene to help all of us? After all, when you analyse the events both leading up to and after, valuable lessons have been learned by not only me but hopefully Karen, Mark and Brian.

This time I have spent in the house on my own has made me realise I can exist on my own but, more importantly, it has taught me being on your own does not fulfil life because life is all about sharing, communicating. It is about loving, laughing, and helping each other to cope with life's problems. Anyway, Brian has not apologised for spitting at me and I do wish he would not for the reasons you are thinking of i.e. respecting ones Father, no I am afraid my reason is a lot deeper. You see when someone dies you always wish you could have said “I am sorry for this” or “I didn't mean to say that”. When I die one thing that will throw up in Brian's mind “I wish I could have told my Dad I am sorry for that

My only wish for my children is that it does not take those many years to learn that being caring, and showing love, is not a sign of weakness but is in truth the key that opens the door to give you the ability to give love without looking for anything in return.
I would also like Brian to know that his action of spitting at me was not his fault but mine. I should have been able to reach out and give him more love to help him through the trauma but I hope he realises and more importantly, understands that I am human and the strain I was under was immense as well. Not having love in your life or the feeling of being wanted, needed, makes life in itself pointless.

It is quite strange sitting here writing all this knowing that the only time it may be read will be by my children who will learn their own lessons in life but can hopefully learn something from this.

These experiences I have shared for you are not written for sympathy. On the contrary, I have in my life been very lucky to have experienced 16 years of love with a woman who I can call my friend and I hope one day we can be together again. I have three lovely children who I wish for them only that they experience true love like their Mum and Dad enjoyed. Please remember men and women are all born, with one ability and that is the ability to change, but change has to come from within. By changing to become a better person affects many others in so many other ways that can affect the future for the better. And change we must, if only to stop the present trend where we can so easily explain away the countless wrongs we do. Hiding behind God in whatever religious movement you are a part of, if they think by going to Church every Sunday that they can remove themselves from personal responsibility then they will find out this is just not the case.
In reality, they are going to have to face the truth. In short term, yes they can hide, but as I have said before, it is the future that counts.

We can change the future. Let us be more aware so that we are not easily fooled by slick media that can in one half hour programme give the impression that our Government who cares so much that they want air strikes because 17 people died in a market somewhere in Bosnia. But all the troubles that terrorists have caused in and around the world that are known to them that they simply say it's terrible. Yes, it is! very shocking that so few very bad people can get away with affecting so many good people's lives and get away with it time after time.

It is time to stop all this madness, the double standards in life where Governments can tell the people "No you can't have a pay rise" but continually award themselves higher than the rate of inflation. They say one parent families are scrounging. As a one parent family myself I wish my partner was with me, that would allow me to get involved back in a working environment.

I hate, with a passion, those that play with people's minds and their emotions. I personally have never done this and can't understand why so many do it on a moment to moment basis. Why can't you be truthful with someone? Don't tell someone that you love them when you don't. Be truthful with someone and they will be truthful with you. Both religion and politics are two subjects I hate with a passion because both are about controlling people's minds, their emotions and getting away with the very thing that they are preaching for the masses not to do. The prime example of that is that we have a Bishop who not only fathered a child and lied about it but the very Church that has struck fear into thousands and thousands of ordinary people have not only covered it up but have kept him employed.

The mainstream churches from Evangelical, Salvation Army, Catholic and all orthodox churches have all shared in some scandal. This has not been written to judge them. On the contrary, it is written so that they may and must judge themselves in regards to the way they judge others and in fact, if they logically think about it, how they can judge homosexuality, spiritualists or any others for that matter that do not fit in their system. Life is filled with many different groups of people with varying degrees of wisdom and knowledge. It is about time all religions recognised that we are all different, that we are all at different learning stages and many search to find where they are most suited to. If it means that they practice a different religion from you don't castigate them or exclude them, as long as each individual has found their own God within themselves. In fact, let us unite in facing the real problems that face us today; homelessness, starvation. I am not talking about third world countries. I am talking about closer to home. Let us go back to the simple values in our lives that when your neighbour is in trouble we all help. It is little wonder that a high kirk member in this day and age is expelled for going to a Catholic funeral. It is about time people stopped hiding behind the Church because in reality they are only bigots, but we are all to blame for letting them get away with it. As I have said earlier, life is full of little surprises and none more so than the message I received on 29th March 1994. Now before I go any further I would like to point out that the initials and some names have been changed to protect the people's identity. The reason that I wrote down all of my messages will become exceptionally clear to everyone who reads this because if you are told something and you try and retain that information, you then put your own slant on it i.e. the medium said this or the medium said that . I did not want that ever to be the case. I wanted to write down exactly what was given to me by God and Spirit. And if you think about this logically, once again, it makes life easier to understand why these messages are given.

We the divine will go to any lengths to let you all know we are here for everyone.

It is God's way of saying "I am here for everyone, for all of you just ask and thou shall receive". It is also in part a great lesson to be learnt from having faith in what you have been told and having faith that God and Spirit are a reality.

The message I received on 29th March 1994 was not exceptionally long. It simply said, and I was told that a woman with a capital M A would be entering my life and something good would happen in May. End of message. On the face of it there wasn't a great deal to look into at that point and once again, as I have said throughout all of this book, I always write everything down, so duly noted this and quickly forgot it.

Here is one of the most important lessons I have learned from the divine and has been given to me to share by them.
What you do with the information is down to you all as individuals. What you decide to do with it will determine if you have listened and more importantly understood the lesson!

Do not live your life around the messages we give you all, as the reasons We (The Divine) give you is to help and give you an understanding and an awareness that their truly is a Divine spiritual world that awaits your return if we touch your life it is only to open up the unconditional Love and Forgiveness whilst here on the earth dimension

As Mark was now out of care and back living with me all my energies were being directed towards him, taking him walks, swimming and playing snooker. I was also told that I would be out of this house by the end of the summer. Just small pieces of a jigsaw, but God's subtle plan to let me know the depths of His love not only for me but for everyone that is willing to seek and find the answers. The chain of events I am about to detail is so enormous it takes my breath away as I sit and write them on this Saturday, 3rd September 1994.

As I said, Mark was home. The next fight I had to undertake was to get Brian home and working closely with the social work another valuable lesson learned here… work with them because in reality if you don't your children will be lost in the system forever. The day I got Mark home I had to attend a panel to get them to discharge Mark into my custody. That day, Sandra, who was my new social worker, offered me a lift back into Saltcoats as the Panel hearing was being held in Ardrossan at that particular time. Sandra was also a spiritual lady and I just knew deep within me that God had placed this lady to help, not only me but to help my children as well. On the way back from Ardrossan into Saltcoats Sandra said to me "Robert, can I ask you something?" and I said "Of course you can". She said "I am going into hospital shortly are you picking up anything as I am really concerned?"
I said "You will be fine Sandra, don't worry". "That's not from Spirit" I said, "That's from me". "You will be alright". And as I said that I got a terrific pain in my ankle. I said "Are you in pain with your ankle?" She said "No", but it was real and I felt it so I knew it was either there or going to happen so I thought to myself I will not pursue it. I said my goodbyes and arranged for her to call the following week. When she did not appear I thought nothing of it until the following week, so I called at the local office to learn that she had been out walking with her dog in Arran and she slipped and fell down a hill resulting in her ankle being very badly broken. In fact, it was shattered, resulting in her being air lifted to Crosshouse Hospital where she has been for some time.
April came and went and May opened it's door. I was still attending my Church meetings in Irvine on a Sunday evening. The sheer peace of mind and the feeling I get from being able to reach out and touch people's lives, not only through being able to give them a message but also through the healing side of it, has given my life so much purpose I cannot adequately describe to you in words how grateful to God I truly am. To me this was another Sunday evening, 15th May 1994; this was to be the beginning of some immense lessons for me, as I have already stated it has literally taken my breath away

How God does truly work in mysterious ways is a pleasure to behold when the full picture is revealed to you.
The meeting finished and Mark and I returned home, Mark said "can I get some chips Dad?" I said "Okay do you want to go down the town to Vincent's Chip Shop (his chips are truly excellent)?" "No Dad let's just go up the road". There is a chip shop just up from where we lived. I said "Okay" and we started up the road. Three quarters of the way up Mark stopped to pet a dog and a woman appeared from a house and he spoke to the woman.
It turns out she knew Mark as her son had been friends with him. She came over to the fence and said "I saw you at a recent spiritual meeting, do you go a lot?" I said "Yes, every Sunday". I was just about to walk away when I turned and said to her "Who is going to the lawyer this coming Tuesday or in fact Wednesday?" She said "No-one". The colour in her face changed and she said "My sister is". She said "Do you give messages as well?" Mark replied before I opened my mouth "Yes a lot". I said "No not a lot but yes I do from time to time receive some messages". She invited us in for a coffee. I said "No, I am taking Mark for chips he is starving". "Well go and get his chips and come back in on the way down and I will put the kettle on and butter some slices of bread for both of you". I kept trying to get out of it but she was very persistent. I had barely sat down and was aware of a lady present. A photo frame of a lady appeared on the carpet in front of me. I duly described the woman and it was confirmed to me it was in fact her Mother. I then picked up the cancer condition which her Mother had passed away with. The evidence that evening was breath taking, but let me point out that I can take no credit for it then or even now as I posses nothing everything I receive is given to me by the divine. Others would do well to learn this valuable lesson!

Mediums possess nothing everything is given to you by the divine and a lot of Spirit workers Truth.

Another valuable lesson to be learned here and this is for all mediums, healers, empaths. Whatever you receive is given to you and is not from you, put your ego to the side and give of yourself unconditionally without ever looking for anything in return.
We as humans possess nothing, God supplies the information to us so therefore, how can we take credit for something that we in fact do not possess? We only possess the ability once again given to us by the graciousness and the love from God and Spirit to enable us to reach out and help with love, compassion, forgiveness and understanding. Being there for another human being while never looking for anything in return from that individual and if you truly understand this you will feel contentment in your soul that you would have never dreamed at all possible.

I finished my coffee and duly left to go back down the road with Mark. The following evening, her son appeared at my door and asked if I could speak to his Mum's Sister as she was really hurting. I said “Yes, but I can't promise a message, that's Gods will”. A time was duly set in my diary for 8.30pm that evening.
I, in truth, was scared. Not to talk to her but in case no evidence came through for her. Another valuable lesson was to be learned from this fear within and that was God puts you or puts people in your pathway for a reason and you should have the faith and the strength to understand that if He has done so then there is a reason for that to happen.

I will never forget walking up the road with Mark on that particular evening feeling scared not as I said because I was frightened to talk to her sister but once again because I wasn't aware or sure that a message would in fact come through and also I thought at the time 'how can the evidence from the evening previous be equalled?'. How wrong I truly was. Another valuable lesson learned. God will go to any length to make people aware there is a spiritual life to consider.

I arrived at the duly appointed time. We exchanged hello to each other and sat in the downstairs front room with a coffee. Again, I had no sooner sat down and their Mum stepped forward.

Again, the evidence was breath taking but personalised to her. I suddenly heard a tune in my head and started to hum it not knowing the title. She just burst out crying. It was her Mum's favourite piece of music which she used to play on the piano for her. I was asked after this to talk to her third Sister the following Monday. I had finished giving off when I sat comforting the Sister in tears. Did I want a coffee? I said "Yes please (to protect their identify I have not named them). As I sat drinking my coffee the relief and the pain was being lifted off them. I was happy for them. Their Christian names were, once again changed to protect them, Mary-Ann (the first lady I had spoken to out in the garden), her sister Mary (who I spoke to on the Tuesday evening) and her third sister Elaine (who I was to speak to the following Monday). At that moment the door opened and in walked the lady's son. He sat down with Mark and started to make fun of the 'spooky spirits'. Just at that the Mum (his Gran) turned me round and with a finger pointing said "enough!" just the way she had always said to him. He turned white and again I was given information that was special to him i.e. describing his bedroom, the toys his Gran had bought for him. It transpires he was giving his Mum a real hard time. I think he got the message.

His Gran who was in spirit! Then said to me," Ask my Daughter out". I replied through thought with no word spoken "I can't do that". You see I take my work very seriously. You cannot play with people's minds or their emotions. There was no further discussion between us.

The following Monday I met the third Sister. Again, it was personalised to her. Her mum said to me "Ask my daughter out". I said "No I can't and will not do that".

The sister said to me "What's up Robert? you look perplexed". I said "Oh nothing I was just thinking about something". The conversation stopped and out of the silence my Son said to his friend "I am lucky to have my Dad". The lady said "How's that Mark?" me sitting there wondering what he was going to say

He then started to tell them back in March we were out walking, Mark, Brian and I at the rocks at the harbour behind the labour club, when I fell and banged my head and he told them how a woman came out with a blanket and wrapped me up and an ambulance was called. I played it down mainly because I was embarrassed as I had told them to be careful and here I was the one that ended up in hospital. Again the divines plan carefully weaved into what to me was normal life but in fact was arranged by the Divine. Anyway, soon after Mark and I left with "Thanks very much Robert" ringing in my ears, I simply said "Don't thank me, thank God, it is His love for you that you have been granted a message of not only hope but comfort". As Mark and he were friends I was invited up for a coffee every evening after that, not only enjoying this lady's company but also both her Sisters' company. One evening this lady turned, looked over her shoulder at me and it was as if a bullet had hit me straight between the eyes. I because of my strong principles dismissed it from my mind. I thought this is now the right time to say that the work with the family was complete and it was time for me to help someone else. We now have reached the beginning of June and one of the Sisters said "Could you talk to my friend Maryellen, give her a message?" I said I would certainly talk to her but I cannot promise a message. A date was set, Thursday 9th June, the day before Marks birthday. I was introduced to her again in this lady's house and sure enough I had hardly got comfortable when her grandfather had stepped forward and duly gave me a lot of information about her, but it was Maryellen's Mother most of the message was for and a lot of names came forward but Maryellen did not know them.

I was given a description of her Mother's home and this was confirmed to me to be accurate by Maryellen.

I said I felt her Mother felt very lonely and to tell her Father walked beside her and he gave me a description of himself. The message duly ended when Maryellen announced to me in front of the three Sisters, Mark and his friend that she had picked up something from me, so I dared her to tell me.

She said "I can't, not in front of everyone". Thinking she was bluffing I said

“Excuse us while Maryellen and I go through to the kitchen”. She said “Robert you are very fond of this lady but you are torn because you still have love for your Wife”. I was stunned, she was right! but I said “Even if I could - I was fond of her – I couldn't go out with her as it was not morally the right thing to do, to go out with a person that I have given a message to”. She smiled and replied “I know you will be good for her and treat her with respect”. She also said “Why run away from happiness? You are human and you are a very nice person”. I cut the conversation and went in and said my goodbyes. The lady phoned later and asked if everything was alright. I said “Yes”. “Come up tomorrow night for a coffee” she said, I made an excuse I couldn't make it. She said “Well come up Saturday night”, I said “okay". Saturday came around and again sitting in the front room I was pressed by this lady what had happened on Thursday while talking to Maryellen. I tried and tried to change the subject but eventually I was backed into a corner. I said “I think it would be better if I did not see you again”. She was shocked and confused thinking she had done something wrong. I said “You have done nothing wrong, it's me”. I then had to explain I had developed feelings for her as we had not been out of each other's company since that Sunday night, 15th May. I got up, apologised and went to leave. The lady said “Please sit-down Robert. I was not aware Robert you had these feelings for me”. I became totally embarrassed and again I apologised. “There is no need to Robert” she said “Can I sit on your knee for a minute?” Thinking she was feeling sorry for me. I went to get up but she sat on my knee and kissed me. We kissed for five hours and eventually watched the sun come up.

The following Tuesday I was doing a training platform with Margaret Dreyer and told her how guilty I felt becoming involved with someone I had given a message to. Margaret, in her own unique style, said “You are not God Robert you are human. It was not your intention to get involved, Spirit set this up”. These words 'spirit set this up' which was said casually by Margaret at the time did not realise that in fact they had set it up for not only my benefit but for this lady's benefit as well. Another valuable lesson on my part had been learned. Yes, I have the ability to feel all these emotions inside me that I thought died along with my wife in 1991. Yes, I have learned how lonely and boring my life is without female company, to sit and have a coffee and exchange conversation. How wonderful life really is with these simple pleasures. God does work in mysterious ways. The woman who wrapped the blanket round me and cuddled me until the ambulance came turned out to be Maryellen's Mum. Another valuable lesson learned. If you reach out and touch and help someone God will truly repay you, maybe not in monetary value, but I was allowed through God to repay that lady with giving her a message which helped her through a difficult period in her life.

I hear you asking "And what about this lady and you?". We went to Blackpool, separate beds (with the boys Christopher and Mark) but sadly it did not work out. This lady is going out with someone else but I will always be eternally grateful to her for making me feel alive again and at least I tasted for a short spell, happiness, thank you very much.

Brian started to come home and the tension between the two brothers erupted one evening with Brian smashing the bathroom mirror and trying to get to Mark with it, trying to kick his door in to get him. Needless to say, both ended up in care again. To me it was never ending, just one thing after another. I had been asking social work for months and months to refer them both to professional counselling, all the time falling on deaf ears. It was suggested by me I take Brian home to try and stabilise him as he was totally out of control in the home. Swearing at staff was bad but he also assaulted a woman member of staff resulting in him being charged with assault by the Police, but as he was a minor the only thing was for him to appear before the children's panel where he promptly told them to Fuck Off !. Mark was taken to voluntary care in order for this work to be carried out. It just seemed everything was becoming more and more impossible. I was informed by letter on 16th August 1994 that a review would be held on Mark the following Monday, 22nd August at 2pm in Ardrossan. Monday came so quickly. That morning as I was very tense, I decided to go a walk to the local library for a CD. My cousin's wife Anne-Marie works there, and when I went to the counter she said "We phoned you last night". I said "Brian and I went for a game of snooker is everything okay?". She went white and said "You haven't heard then?". I said "Heard what?". Uncle Tom died over the weekend, he gets buried tomorrow". As my Dad was with my Sister in Basingstoke, I said I would represent him. I just burst out crying. Ann-Marie said "I am sorry you had to find out this way".

Before I knew it 2pm approached. Mark was late. We started the Panel hearing without him. He eventually came in. I sat there thinking about my Uncle Tom's Wife and how does it happen to such lovely caring people.

The Panel I thought was going to be predictable in as much as I would express how I felt, what was best for the boys and they would say "fine" and take no heed of what I said. It just goes to show life throws up some surprises. From time to time they asked for my views and I opened by saying "Do you want the truth or do you want me to say what you want me to say". "No Mr Gallacher, please tell us how you view your Son's progression since coming into care". I said "Well he has been taught no values and no respect, he can do anything he wants and he still gets his pocket money. He will be taken away to a leisure centre even though he has been bad. I have asked and asked for months for some professional medical help to be given to both boys but no one will listen. Well let me tell you these two boys were brought up in a loving stable environment. Their Mum and I taught them respect, love, to be caring, to help others. Now all I see is two boys that can do virtually as they please with no corrective action being taken".

At that they turned to the Social Work and said "We understand therapy was being sought for both boys?". "Well it was requested" was the reply. "Well the recommendation is we will ask for it to be carried out”. I simply said in my mind 'thank you God' someone is listening to me at long last.

I came home to be informed by Brian he was suspended for three days. I said “You will have to go to school tomorrow as I have my Uncle's funeral to attend”. I had been aware that I was having trouble with my breathing but didn't think It was too bad.

The following day at the funeral I was in extreme difficulty to the point I thought I was going to have a heart attack. It was that bad. I made it through and decided I would go to the Doctors on my return home. I went down and was seen quite quickly. It was established I had a bad lung infection and was prescribed strong antibiotics. As I was home by myself due to Brian being in the home for two nights being Tuesday and again the following night. I thought I would go to Ayr Church as Gordon Smith was on. A good spirit worker is Gordon. I duly took off my black tie and replaced it with a more colourful tie. I got the bus at Saltcoats station and enjoyed the bus trip to Ayr which takes one and a half hours. I thought, selfishly, I would go for a message to give me some hope, some light at the end of my tunnel.

I was greeted by Gordon, who shook my hand firmly and warmly and with a big smile said “How are you Robert? Can you help me?”. I said “Yes what is it?”. “Can you share platform with me as I need to leave early”. I could not refuse although in truth I was a wreck myself, what with the funeral, my own health, the problems with my two sons. Another valuable lesson I learned very young, it does not matter how bad you are feeling there is always someone worse off and to that end God has given me the ability to touch people's lives. So there must be a reason for him asking me to share the platform, I agreed. I was due to do a training platform with Margaret Dreyer the following week at this very church. I opened in prayer, Gordon gave the address and went onto clairvoyance straight away. I sat there inhaling olbas oil to help me to breathe asking God to lift this condition off me when it was time for me to get up. Before I knew it Gordon was finished and was saying goodbye. I was asked if I wanted a couple of minutes. I said

“No I will go straight up”. Spirit drew me to this woman at the back of the hall and made me aware she was an only daughter or she only had one daughter. This was confirmed and the rest of the information followed. I then, after some time with this woman, was drawn to a lady some three rows in front and I again gave information I was given. Everything was fine until my concentration was broken by people leaving as it was close to time. I made an apology and said in truth that was all I received and sat down. I travelled home by bus and was sitting there tired, drained. I simply said “Please God give me a good night's sleep.
God did grant me a peaceful night's sleep and as there is a reason for everything. I thought I am going to need my strength the following day, Wednesday. Again, my inner spirit was right. I had just finished a cup of tea when the phone rang out. I picked it up and it was Brian's school. The Headmaster informed me that Brian had in fact been suspended for five weeks minimum and I would receive a letter to come in and discuss the situation. I knew in my heart that it was going to be bad news particularly since Brian was only back at school two weeks since he was accepted back into the school, that they more or less were going to expel him, him and Mark, if their behaviour did not get better. I knew they would not stand for any more nonsense and my worst fears were confirmed. The following week at the meeting with the school it would appear that Brian turned round and told the teachers including the Head Teacher, to “go away” but not as polite as that. I immediately asked Brian that all concerned be given an apology as his Mum and myself had brought him up to respect his elders.
I apologised on his behalf and asked him to apologise to the teachers he said will I Fuck!... and stormed out of the door.

The pain as I sit and write this is so immense that with this pain comes again lessons in respect you can give your children love, support them, teach them right from wrong, good from bad, but the reality is they will make their own mind up as to how they want their life to go…

Do not spend your time beating yourself up over your children's behaviour.

As long as you have installed values and morals into them your job is complete.

It is then down to themselves how they live their lives as once again you don't know what your child's journey is all about!

The day after the school meeting a letter from the reporter dropped through my door. The report had to be compiled on Brian for the assaults he carried out and a Panels hearing would be set up. I fear the worst that Brian may end up in Residential Care. God please help me but more importantly help him.

The following day the man from the mortgage company called and informed me that they were about to start repossession of the house. I sat there thinking to myself… 'lucky white heather, has anyone got some?' After he left I sat alone crying, I again realised another lesson. You see this was the house that Mary, my Wife, wanted. It is now time for another chapter in my life to be closed. Yes, it is very painful, 16 years of working very hard, sharing good times as well as bad times, that's called true love. It shows very graphically that life really does exist literally from minute to minute and we take so much for granted. Knowing that things always come in threes I wondered 'what next?' I was stunned when Margaret Dreyer picked me up and said "I went down like a lead balloon at Ayr! She explained people complained to her that I spent 20 minutes with one woman. To say I was gutted and felt sick to the pit of my stomach is no exaggeration. Not as you may think because my pride had been hurt, but I said earlier that God would go to any length to make man and woman realise that they have a spiritual life. Obviously that message is not getting through in the churches. Yes, I know I am just a new face in the door but if God gave me all the information as He did it was because this particular lady needed it that evening. I have always asked the divine because I know that the spiritual dimensions are real and so to give me quality information before quantity so that the person receives the information goes away not thinking but knowing the information could come from no other source other than from the divine realms.

I had been given my address from Spirit over the weekend prior to the meeting but Margaret said "Just go up cold Robert and speak from your heart Robert, as you do with me". Margaret said the opening prayer and before I knew it I was standing in front of all those people who had come from all different backgrounds and for many different reasons. I asked if there was anyone here for the first time and there was quite a lot this particular evening. I extended a warm welcome and said "For many of you this evening is a voyage of personal discovery and there will be one person this evening that has come for the same reason, as I did for walking through the doors for the first time which for me was my Wife at the age of 34 had passed to spirit. Like many here this evening I had lost direction. I was hurting, I was frightened, I had died the night my Wife died, but I have found, as I hope you will find, the strength in this movement is not the people who stand up here. It is not about Margaret Dreyer and to an even lesser extent me. It is about the people sitting around you who have suffered and been given the strength to help other people in spite of the hurt they are feeling. I would like to give you a graphic example of that. Last Monday I was informed my Uncle had died, my Son Mark was taken into care because he couldn't cope with his Mother's death. My other son was suspended for three days, just another Monday I thought. Tuesday, I buried my Uncle and thought, very selfishly

I would come to Ayr Church as Gordon Smith was on and a good spirit worker he is. I thought maybe spirit could give me a bit of a lift as I had a bad lung infection as well, but only that day discovered this as I had to go to the doctors after the funeral because I could hardly breathe. When I walked through the door Gordon asked me if would do him a big favour by helping him on the platform as he had to leave early. With no thought of myself or my problems I said yes. I did not stand up here for ego or for money. I only want to give back what God gave to me and that is peace of mind and in my darkness he sent Margaret Dreyer and Sally Buxton to my aid. The greatest gift God can give anyone is the ability to reach out and help someone even when your own life seems to be falling apart. I do not need a platform to do this, I deal every day and, in fact, all my life I have been there when I was needed. I do not want to thanked. I do not want to put up on a pedestal because in truth Robert Gallacher is not important. What is important though is the realisation that there are many people out there needing help, needing support, that today so many people are unwilling to give. What in essence is life in itself? It is about caring for each other. I took criticism for spending too long with one person. I make no apology for that because in truth it meant that the person really needed it. I would like to thank each and every one for listening and may God grant each person here this evening, at some point in your lifetime, peace of mind".

I was given a round of applause which, in truth, baffled me. You see, I only speak the truth. The lady came to me that I had given the message to the week before and said yes she did really need it and thanked me. I said, as I always do "Thank God, not me, I just gave you what He gave me to give to you" Another truth. I don't really understand. I was given the ability or gift. All I know is it helps people to come to terms with death and gives them the strength to pick up the pieces of their own lives, and God promised he would comfort the bereaved and in His House there were many Mansions. My only wish is more people could be helped as I have been. This experience is of course human nature, which more people would want a message but as I have always been very sensitive it has left me wondering whether I would do platform work again. What has this world become when the indifference to each other has overtaken the simple truth that we not only need each other we are interdependent on each other. Why can people be so blind to that simple truth?

Margaret gave me an update on Karen, as I said previously, she had moved in with her in her home in Beith, Margaret did not need to take her in but she did so out of love and compassion for our situation. Margaret made me aware that what I said about Karen's behaviour in the past and leading up to her moving out and moving in with Margaret was the Truth!! I again in truth was hurt within as Margaret was Spiritual and was supposed to be very aware and should have known that I was telling the truth! Another valuable lesson learned here was that most claim and say they are very aware is in fact not the case!! anyway Margaret said Karen's behaviour was steadily getting worse and she was rebelling against Margaret's house rules. I said to her ask Karen if she wanted to come back home the words were not finished out of my mouth and Margaret said I said to her the other night if she does not want to live by the house rules you can go back to your Dads and followed that up by saying she has moved in with a boy in Paisley!! End of conversation.

My son Brian and I walked through Saltcoats town centre the following evening on route to play snooker and I met Mr Hilton and his daughter Jean. We stood talking and Brian said something smart. I just turned and said to him "The reason Mr Hilton liked me so much when I was younger was because of the way that I would always be polite and courteous" and how life has changed so very much. Mr Hilton replied "You know Bobby, years ago when I would take you out for a run in the car and we would go up to the dump to burn papers and nothing was ever thought about it because in those days people cared for each other, but today you would be thought to be strange 'to have a relationship' with a young boy who was not related to you". I simply replied "Life, people have changed so much Mr Hilton and it frightens me to say this but the truth is people have lost the ability to care, and I mean genuinely care, about each other. Can we, do we want the change? We must change this trend. I hope in my heart at some point we do".

How do I end this story? Or bring it to a conclusion? Do I tell you a lie and end with a fairy tale ending? I prefer to tell you the truth, and the truth is there is never an ending in life just another blank page that God fills up which then becomes your life experiences, your personal challenges, and your lessons to be learned, to overcome. But remember, whatever happens in your life, God is there and is waiting for you to simply say "Please God help me". If you say this from your heart, your soul, God will open the door that will give you the direction you need in your life. however big the problem may be or seem it will be sorted. Please believe me. If anyone reads this, I hope in your lifetime you receive peace of mind as I have done and may God bless you with seeing the beauty in the simple things in life, being able to share your life, your love, with someone without ever looking for anything in return from that person. Keep the faith and touch someone's life that may be feeling worse than you, and remember God will repay you with peace of mind.

The house was repossessed and Brian and I were moved into a hostel, again it was heart-breaking walking away from the house. I heard through the grapevine that Karen was living with a boy she had met at the sea cadets in Paisley. While at the hostel Brian and I managed to get a cheap deal to Butlin's in Bognor Regis and the hostel was right next to the train station in Ardrossan. We only had to walk about fifty feet and we were on the train. As we were living in the one room together 24/7 it was at times very tense as Brian was very volatile with mood swings, but I thought this will do him the world of good getting away from the room we seemed to be trapped in. I knew he loved Butlin's and would disappear all day long only returning for something to eat at meal times so I thought this would be perfect for him. We arrived and he was angry!... and I thought I have had enough of this and told him we would travel back home the following morning, he disappeared for a couple of hours and then returned calmed down so we spent the

Monday to Friday there. I never really saw him much as he would go off and make friends. When we first arrived, we were told this was a one parent family week and we were all to meet up the following morning and introduce ourselves, we could meet as a group either for dinner or out to the shows, it was very relaxed. Brian said that would be great for you Dad so I went and we all got along really well and decided we would all meet up that night for the show and drinks after. I was sat with the group and sat next to a lady called Janet she was from Harrogate and she had a son called Sam and so Brian was introduced to her son and the two of them got on fine. Sam was a really nice lad so him and Brian just went and done their own thing for the rest of the week. Janet and I hit it off right away and I don't mean as an item, so we spent the week together in the group and even went out to a Spiritualist Church in Bognor together as she had just lost her friend to cancer only a few weeks earlier. The week went very quickly and before we knew it we were saying our goodbyes and Janet gave me her phone number and asked me to phone her over the weekend to let her know we arrived back home safe and sound. The journey home was a long one via the train and Brian was getting more and more tense. I kind of guessed it was because we were going back to our one room in the Hostel. We made it back and Brian's temper flared again. He walked out of the hostel and in truth I did not know when he was going to come back. A couple of days later he arrived back, seemingly he had stayed with a friend. I was so relieved to see him I just hugged him. I was now at the stage I did not say anything in case he got angry and blew up again. I became more and more withdrawn in myself blaming myself over and over again telling myself if I had taken my life their Mum would be there and they all would be happy without me. So in my eyes and more importantly in my own mind everything was my fault. I had failed at being a good Husband. I was still alive and Mary was gone. If I had been successful in taking my own life because I loved them all so very much God would have taken care of them. All I knew deep inside I had Failed as a Father also! To do the thing that was to me very simple, to guide and protect them.

Being an empath comes at a huge price as you pick up on how everyone feels around you and know what they are thinking and all you want to do is take their pain away from them but you can't.

God works in mysterious ways and it was not my time but Mary's time and to her Mum and her Sisters. I am sorry that Mary is not here today and again I cannot take their pain or anger away from them. You see I have never had the opportunity to let them know how much I loved her as they don't talk to me and before you ask are you having a dig at them the truth is no. What I am saying is sorry to them that I am here and Mary is not, but all their questions will be answered in the fullest of time.

I remember receiving a message in Kilmarnock church and was told to go to my Mother in law and deliver it personally. Apprehensive was an understatement as in truth she never really liked me, but undaunted I went this one day and she was surprised to see me. I said Cathy I am here to deliver a message.
She said I don't believe anything you tell me. I said Cathy this is not from me but from a medium in Kilmarnock Church who does not know me and said I have to come and tell you if you let go of the anger within you Mary will come back and speak to you to prove she is OK !
I left at that point and the following week when I attended the church I was pulled to the side and was told that I was to stop frightening people. She said she had met her friend Cathy in the town centre and she was talking about me. Little did this woman know this same Cathy was in fact my mother- in- law.
I never made her aware, but drew her attention to the fact that the message never came from me but from a medium the week before in this very church!! Some couple of months later Sunday morning on Mother's Day the phone rang it was Cathy to say Robert I was standing at the sink peeling potatoes when I heard Mary shout my name. I am so excited I had to phone you first. I have not even told the girls yet. I went back to the church and approached the lady to let her know that what I was given was in fact the Truth and did happen!! Did I get an apology? No...
Another valuable lesson learned is Trust in God and Spirit as they

will never let you down but Humans always will let you down Truth!

I used to attend this church on a regular basis and after that I stopped going. Again, for every action there is a reaction and she just made me feel uncomfortable. But I never held any bad feeling to her or the church as I just put it down to another lesson learned. When you are not motivated by money or ego it frees the soul to fulfil its purpose here on earth. Allowing you to give of yourself your love without ever looking for anything in return.

We the divine will take you out of a situation we do not want you to be in! You have never taken things personally as you know there is a good reason why you are not meant to be there and you never question it. To Love and forgive unconditionally keeps you from needless drama and gives you such peace of mind as you don't allow someone else to live in your mind.

Soon after Brian and I returned back Janet offered us a chance to visit her and stay with her and Sam which we duly did. Brian's temper once again got the better of him and he hit Sam which resulted in Sam coming in crying and when asked what happened he explained that he was with Brian and some of his mates were making fun of his accent, Sam laughed and Brian hit him. I sat in his room comforting Sam and was trying to explain that Brian had been through a lot over the past couple of years but I was not making any excuses for him.

Brian returned back at the house a couple of hours later. I spoke with him and told him that was not nice thing to do especially as they had put us up and given us a wee much needed break. He did apologise to Sam and I felt so proud of him as there was signs that the loving caring boy Mary and I had brought up was starting to show a wee glimmer of hope of returning back to the boy that once was.

We returned home as it was only for the weekend Janet and I kept in touch but Brian and I never went back down together again. About 2 months after being back at the hostel Brian was missing his brother and so the cycle began all over again. Brian joined Mark in residential care I was still attending meetings trying to get them back. In Truth I knew it was never going to happen but yet another lesson was being given and that was from the divine.

The harder you all fight against change the more the Pain continues until the lesson is learned and understood. And for some they will never embrace the change because change frightens them and that includes in relationships where we see couples living together in misery rather than be honest and truthful with one another and if they were they could move on and experience new lessons, While remaining good friends and feel grateful to one another that lessons were learned on both sides if two people grow together then there is no problem it is when one grows spiritually and the other one is perhaps at different growth stage from the other person as everyone develops at different paces but if you learn to be honest and truthful with one another and Love and

Forgive Unconditionally it allows the other person to grow at their own pace and that might just be enough for the relationship to rekindle in the future instead of the destructive behaviour we see today from name calling to using children as pawns in their personal battles.

I was not prepared or ready to give up on the boys who I loved with my whole being and still and always will. Not long after Brian was taken into residential care I was offered a house in Fleming Crescent, Saltcoats which was not that far from Dalry road where I was brought up. I went to the wee local church a few days before the house offer was made and again God was giving me answers to try and ease all my fears and worries. But the impending thought of where will I end up how will I afford to do the house up as I still clung to getting the boys back with me at some point, where would I find money to get carpets down as Brian also suffered with asthma for a period of time and I would need to keep it as dust free as possible. I could not bear to watch and go through what I witnessed with Mary dying in front of me and being put on life support even now all these years later. I cannot sit and watch someone on television getting shocked back to life I find it takes me back to seeing Mary laying there her face blue. Yes, the mind is a very powerful thing!!

The message simply said there is a house move coming very soon and don't panic you will be given a lot of help and as I said I was told this about four days before the offer was made known to me.

In fact the social worker turned up the following afternoon and said I am taking you for a drive as I have some news for you.

What is the old saying we the divine told you all thousands of years ago! There is none so blind that cannot see!

I hope that when anyone reads this they do not feel sympathy for me or in fact the children. Yes I cannot deny it was very tough for the children and even more so for me as I could not do anything to change the lessons that we all had to go through, which hopefully will open up your mind to becoming aware that the divine and the spirit world are real and God will go to any lengths to make mankind aware. This is yes a human existence and a school house of learning but we must prepare for the spirit world as time here on earth is a very short time and we cannot take money, bonds jewellery, cars or houses with us. When our time comes it is the love and forgiveness you give to each one that touches your life That is what we all are truly measured by.

The social worker said we can go and look through the window as I don't have the keys as they are working on getting it ready for you. This was now 1993 I was so excited with many things running through my mind. It meant I could get the opportunity to get the boys back. I was getting out of a room in the hostel where there was only four white painted walls, would I manage to decorate it to make it a home for Mark and Brian and no I had not forgot my first-born Karen. In fact she was never off my mind, but she decided she did not want anything to do with me and she was living in Paisley and I learned she was pregnant, and as I can tell the truth knowing full well that I will go to my grave without ever seeing her or my grandchildren and you will understand why I can state that with truth as you read on. I was angry and disappointed in her for getting pregnant as she was in the sea cadets and the boys and I done without, so she would have enough to go on all the courses with the sea cadets. Her officer came to see me and said Karen has a wonderful career in front of her in the navy and she is officer material and I have no doubt she will go far. As he was telling me this my heart was pounding out my chest with pride and love that I so wished her Mum could be here, to see her grow and unfold as the beautiful rose she was.

Yes I did get a lot of help via social work to enable the boys to return home and that included a team of offenders coming in to paint the house for me which was part of their community service , She arranged a grant which enabled me to buy wallpaper and curtains and because of Brian's health needs a grant for carpets and at the time a friend was selling wardrobes and I asked could I get them and I would pay for them over a number of weeks. They both agreed so everything seemed to be falling into place.
I was visiting Mark and Brian in Kerelaw School and they seemed to be doing ok, in the sense that they could talk to one another without fighting with each other, well it appeared that way.
The house finally took shape and the social work approached me with a view to taking Brian out of care and staying with me gradually before full return to live permanently with me. Brian would come for the odd night and this expanded as the weeks went on again it was good days and bad days but we had made a start!

I joined a one parent group it was held in a centre behind Wheatly Road shops, it was as it says on the tin- a one parents meeting place, learning new skills going out to bowling at a local centre. We also went to Harvies which consisted of a swimming pool and ice rink where we were given an introduction to curling on the ice. Having only seen it done on television my thought was how hard can this be throwing a stone along ice to reach the other end… how wrong was I!! they were heavy and the first couple of attempts broke the ice (pardon the pun) with the group as they fell about laughing at my attempts at launching this stone down the ice. The session lasted for a couple of hours and we all had a great time. We had a community bus with a driver and an instructor who would accompany us where we went and would always finish back at the centre for 3PM so a couple of parents could collect their younger children from the crèche. Funding had been provided for this by the local government, it was just before the cuts were being introduced and fortunately we had funding for the next 18 months in place as we were considered an urban aid fund area. That would take us through till 1995, for me it was a god send and gave me a chance to meet other one parents, have a chat and a laugh. We would go on various activities from horse riding at local riding centre in Stevenston, we were also given a chance to go Skiing at the dry slopes in Newmilns. We even went abseiling and to badminton. The events were always interesting and fun and we had to make a small contribution towards some events but it was not enough to put pressure on us due to all of us being on a low income. On one journey back to the centre they asked if any of us had any skills we could share with the group on the weeks we had nothing planned. I offered cooking and baking skills as I had done my trade as a chef / baker many years beforehand. I also said that if required I could give a talk and a demonstration of Spiritual Healing. All the women in the group were all very interested in this. Some of the ladies also said they could offer make- up talks and how to apply it. I laughed and said no! I am not volunteering to have make up applied on my face! They all were teasing me and said I would make a good model. When we arrived back at the centre, I was informed that there was a boy looking for me, she said I think it's your Son. I replied no as Brian was in a secure resident section within the school. I walked up the road and entered by the front door and literally a few moments later the back door was not chapped, but sounded as if it was being kicked in. It was in fact my Brian. I brought him in and said I will make a cup of tea and he said thanks Dad. I knew he should not be at my house as there was a planned structure in place. I had already surmised he had run away.

As we were sitting having a cup of tea the front door was chapped you know that chap when a police officer chaps! Brian was very agitated so I said don't worry I won't tell them you are here. But I will take you back later ok! I went to the door and the officer who knew me well as both boys had absconded from not only the homes but the residential school. Hello I don't suppose you have seen Brian? I explained with my voice that if he has run away he must be very agitated in order to do that, while signalling with my eyes and also explaining he will probably appear here but officer as you know I take the boys back. He smiled and said thank you sorry to disturb you. No problem and thank you officer for coming to me. In other words thanks for allowing me time with Brian to calm him down and you know I will return him. They left and I said to Brian what has been happening? “I don't fucking like it there they are all bastards I want to come home to you Dad”, I got him calmed down knowing full well this would hold back his next visit as by a form of punishment to him from the home. Later I took him down to Kerelaw and spoke with one of the staff who had explained Brian and Mark were fighting and had to be separated. Deep down I knew there would always be friction between them and once again I felt hopeless that I could do nothing to help them both. Brian was allowed the following week on my request as I was trying to ensure him he was loved and trying to stabilise the anger that would erupt literally like the hulk

I was asked by the group if I would give a talk on Spiritual Healing and a demonstration of laying on hands in two weeks time.
I agreed to do so and put together a mini workshop of how Spiritual healing has been done for centuries and was Practised by both the Greeks and the Romans, while pointing out that the Romans were in fact the first to use colour healing and they had built Temples at Thebes

The ancient Egyptians have been recorded to have been using colour for cures and ailments. They worshipped the sun, knowing that without light there can be no life. They looked at nature and copied it in many aspects of their lives. The floors of their temples

were often green - as the grass which then grew alongside the River Nile. Blue was a very important colour to the Egyptians too; the colour of the sky. They built temples for healing and used gems (crystals) through which the sunlight shone. They would have different rooms for different colours. We could perhaps relate our present methods of colour/light therapy to this ancient practice. There are lists on papyrus dating back to 1550 BC of colour "cures".
Their deep knowledge and understanding of the healing powers of the colour rays was so nearly lost when, later on in history, the Greeks considered colour only as a science. Hippocrates, amongst others, abandoned the metaphysical side of colour, concentrating only on the scientific aspect. Fortunately, despite this, the knowledge and philosophy of colour was handed down through the ages by a few. The Chinese also apparently practised Colour Healing. The Nei/Ching, 2000 years old, records colour diagnoses.

I put together this thinking that it was only for the group and I was gob-smacked two weeks later to find over 20 people crammed into the room. There were people there I did not know. One lady who had come with her daughter came up at the end and asked if I had any notes, I could give her as she was really interested. I said no I am sorry I didn't expect to be so many here but if I get a chance I will ask the girls in the centre if they could do a photo copy of them for you and to pop back in a couple of days time. At that she said where do you live? I said I have just recently moved into Fleming Crescent, she said, I just live down from there in Boyd Orr road. I explained when I was a youngster, I used to jump from the window out of the house right next to the lane into a big pile of sand as I was brought up and lived in Dalry Road just around the corner. She then said if you manage to get any copies could you perhaps drop them into me. I said no problem as I passed her front door on my way home from the shops anyway.

About a few days later the girls at the centre said I have made some photocopies of your talk you gave Robert. I said thanks very much, I will hand a copy into a lady that was here with her

Daughter. Who was that she said? I said I think her first name is Morag. She said yes Morag works here at the crèche as a helper. She was supposed to be in today, but phoned in as she has had some personal stuff to do and would be out till about 6:30 pm.
I said ok thanks I will pop them through her door then.
She replied Morag would like to thank you as all the women were saying how interesting it was so I am sure she will have a few questions for you! Ok, I will hand them in later to her as I have nothing planned anyway and off, I went home made myself dinner and watched the news with a cup of tea

I took a walk around the corner to where she stayed and chapped the door. she opened the door and looked surprised. I said, "I am sorry but it's just to hand in some notes that you asked for", Come in Morag said, I said "no I don't want to disturb you" but she insisted. She had a friend there and I said, "look you have company I will leave you in peace". she said it's my friend sit down and I will make you a cup of tea. "Ok thanks" and off she went into the kitchen.
Her friend said awe your Robert sarcastically and I replied yes I am. Morag has done nothing but rant and rave about this guy who gave a Healing /Spiritual talk.
I looked down at the floor wishing it would open up and consume me as that was not the reason it was done. It was merely to share and make people aware that healing is not just about going to the doctors, healing can take many forms. Just as Morag came back through with the tea her friend said I think it's a lot of shit! Morag's face went pure red as her friend continued to make me feel very uncomfortable. I drank the tea as fast as I could and said I need to go making excuses that someone was coming to see me. Do you have a phone number she said as I wanted to ask about a couple of things? I said yes here it is she wrote it down.

I left thinking what have I done to her friend that she would be so nasty to me… lesson time.

Another valuable lesson here for you
all to learn and that is you can pick your friends
but you will always encounter those that
don't sit comfortably in your company.
That is not your fault... it is your intuition
working within (Spirit)
It is our way of making you aware that
they are not part of your journey and either
God or the spirit or both within will remove you
from that situation as they are not as developed
or as aware as we have made you.
Therefore, they will not understand you.
It is not a case of they don't like you
but they will see in you something that is missing
in their lives and will allow that human emotion
to overtake them.
and that is jealousy it does not matter to them
that they could learn a lot from you as they are
not at the learning stage that would allow them to
embrace and more importantly understand that
you are a pure vessel of unconditional love and
forgiveness with no hidden agendas with only one
desire and that is to be there for them without
ever looking for anything in return.

Round about 10 pm the phone went it was Morag, she wanted to know what I was doing tomorrow night. As I spent every night in, my diary was not bursting with things or people to see! She said do you fancy coming for a cup of tea tomorrow around 7pm and you could answer some questions I have? So the following evening I went around at the time agreed. She served the tea and said "first I want to apologise for the way my friend spoke to you after you left we had a blazing row about it" I said "Morag don't ruin your friendship on my behalf trust me I have been treated and hurt more by my own family than by strangers, its spirits way of letting you know that they are not part of your journey and they have issues to deal with which they will always reflect onto other people as they can't face the truth about themselves"
I sat talking to her till around 10 pm and then left. I came home made a cup of tea then it was time to be on my own again trying to analyse the chain of events of Mary passing my Mum passing the children being taken into care, just sheer mind tired I went off to bed making no sense of any of it.

This is now 1994 and I keep asking you God for answers, not to question your decisions on me but for me to understand the lessons. I have to learn but more importantly understand. It is now 2016 where all the questions I have had on my mind for the past 60 years have been answered by you as before I was not ready to understand the lessons. And yes, I truly understand them now and it is pleasing to realise that I have recognised for entering the world that I have entered into it with unconditional love and forgiveness and I have not let people destroy that in me…
Thank You Divine Spirit.

I could not find a solution and dosed off.

For every problem there is always a solution! But when you are trapped inside the box it is very hard to find That is why we are opening the boxes for you to understand which will enable you to get our Truth our message heard and enable change each human has to take on board and this will enable you to help so many others in the short time you have left here on this human planet.

The following week the group was on but there was not anything down for this particular day but I went along. It was a real hot sunny day and I arrived waiting for the rest of the group to come. The Mums came and put their children in the crèche so we all went into the room and it was suggested we all go for a walk down the back road to Stevenston and along the high road and back up to the centre. Everyone agreed and the girls in the crèche were asked do you want to bring the children in their prams as that would allow them to get out in the sun, they agreed yes that would be great and as I was coming out the door Morag said "hello Robert". I was taken aback even although I was told she sometimes helps out in the creche. So off we went, we were walking together and she shared her boyfriend had passed away in May 1991 and she had move to Boyd Orr Road in the December of 1991. I said that was the year my Wife had passed. It was a long walk but seemed to go very quickly as we were chatting back and forward and what she was totally unaware of, was I could feel her very sadness which came from the bottom of her soul as I could with everyone I come into contact with! The pain varies from soul to soul depending on the journey they are on and yes sometimes it becomes overwhelming when you can pick up all these feelings and emotions what people are going through. Another valuable lesson I have learned and that again is explained next by the divine.

You cannot take every ones' pain away from them!
You are not God, yes we the divine have put you here with this one mission to Love and Forgive Unconditionally even if some of the lessons are so painful all you really want to do is return home where there is only Unconditional Love ,Forgiveness. And more importantly a deeper understanding of why you go through these human events in your life.
The answer is so very simple it has to do with first and foremost we are Spirit and we return to Spirit,
within the spirit world is many opportunities. Your total spirit existence is not measured or scored with how many friends you have or how much material wealth you have as these and many other earth possessions cannot be taken with you All that returns to spirit is the Love understanding forgiveness you have shown and the lessons that you have learned while here, for many it comes as a total shock to wake up in the spirit world with the knowledge that everything you took on blind faith is in fact an illusion
sometimes it takes many years in the spirit

world to understand and more importantly come to terms with the fact that you have been lied to, so we the Divine have nothing personally to gain by sharing this thought with you!

Look within at the real you face the truth about yourself!!

Change the way you look at things and the way you treat others what you have been told don't accept on blind faith what you are being told because here is a

TRUTH

the world you all live in will not get any better unless you all change it, and that is the paradox!

you must first change yourselves your behaviour not only to yourselves but more importantly to each other. Don't accept what you are being told by someone as being the Truth there is always three sides to a story,

your side, their side and then the Truth!

You may and will lose many valuable friends that have been put here to help you on your journey if you don't understand

Morag invited me down for a cup of tea as she wanted to ask me more questions about lots of things. I never said at any point that I have all the answers but I would always tell her the truth. We would sit till the early hours of the morning discussing all things Spiritual and then I would make my way around the corner to my house.

I made Brian aware that I had a new friendship with a woman he was not happy as you could tell by the way he reacted. I tried to make him aware that it was only a friendship and not a romantic involvement, but I did add and even if it was no one would ever replace his Mother!.

How many reading this have been caught up in the same situation and are saying at this point yes I can relate to this? but we as individuals don't get how our children are feeling and the thoughts that run through their minds which may range from on the surface, I am happy for you both… but what they think in their minds be something quite different.
That could range from awe my Mum or Dad has already forgot my Mother or Father they don't love them anymore or they don't love me anymore as they have someone knew in their life.
These feeling or emotions have to be considered and failure to do so inevitably puts massive strain on the relationships, that changes the dynamics of it as well and leads to the total breakdown with all parties involved. The children may rebel and force one or other to take their side and this quickly leads to tension and frustration.

So having been there and again learned valuable lessons here are answers below given again by the Divine for greater understanding observations on how to look at it differently.
But bearing in mind, if you cannot communicate even at a basic level then these observations will help you to hopefully think outside the box and hopefully be aware before entering a relationship that may in fact be doomed before it has a chance to grow or learn lessons from it.

If you are both entering a relationship the first thing to understand is that you must first sit down and look at the bigger picture especially if children are involved.
You must both agree to be supportive with each other, in other words show and treat each other with respect. The children at the first signs of either rebelling or being cheeky or disrespectful don't tolerate it! Remember you are the Adult and they are the children!! this is the only thing that will give you a chance of making it a success because if allowed just one time to talk to you or your partner with disrespect will result in the child thinking it can divide you both.
Each relationship or friendship is based on everyone that touches your life is a lesson or a blessing, to many relationships end without any lessons being learned from it.
Sadly, this has the knock-on effect of either male or female thinking everyone is the same thus ending each relationship without it ever getting off the ground.
Remember you don't own your children your job is to instil values, morals to teach love, forgiveness, and tolerance as each one is here

*for their own lessons to be learnt.
if you have done this then your job is done.
It is then up to that child to either use those basic foundations you have laid to build upon or not as the case may be as each one will have their own lessons to learn from.*

Over the coming weeks Brian was up one minute and down the next minute and again found himself in residential care all I wanted to do was take his pain away. I felt an absolute failure as the natural thing any parent wants to do is take their child's pain and hurt away from them. With "hindsight" and hindsight is a wonderful thing but no bloody use to you when faced with all these challenges, being on your own is such a burden at times and although having lost my Mum and Mary, having my father still here and Him hurting terribly I could not share my fears with him. As I was supporting him as well, my mind was just on auto and went through the daily routine of hoping and praying that The Divine would intercede and make things better.

Morag was a good support but as she was a single parent herself. I did not want to burden her with what was happening behind the scenes in my life. She would support me and come with me to the children's hearings and meetings I had to attend to try and turn the situation around. But deep in my heart I knew all along I was not going to prevent Brian going through with what he had to experience. I was summoned to a meeting at the social work office in Ardrossan which is in itself strange as after all these years I am staying in a flat across the road from it "Observation" Life is a Circle it just keeps going round and round no matter what we do ! Anyway, Morag came with me and if your mind is becoming aware while reading this you will understand that everything happens for a reason (there is no such thing as coincidence it's a Message from God without a Signature) and again as I was getting ready to go, I could not understand the reason as in truth my mind was full of many unanswered questions. Why did the social work, the school, the Police not check to see if there was any marks or bruises on any of them before just taking them into care. I got a copy of the medical report that was carried out on both the boys when they were taken into care. There were no marks on the boys and why did they not understand you cannot punch someone's teeth out without extensive bruising. Why could these so called professional people not just see we were a family in a crisis with the loss of their Mum ,then six months later their Grandmother (My Mum) the house was being repossessed, I was recovering from a total breakdown and that we all needed support and not for the children to be taken into care. That just kept playing over and over again in my mind. These answers would come much later at the age of 60! As I said, Morag and I attended the meeting and I again expressed that Brian could stay with me but all the values his Mum and I had installed in him seemed to be lost in the anger that sadly Brian was facing himself and clearly struggling with. He will never know how many tears I shed for him (he will now) The meeting started with all who was in the room as they identified themselves on this particular day. There were eight social and care staff present and of course Morag and I. It started at 10am and I thought was going ok until Brian got up off his seat at the top of the table calmly and walked towards me and Morag. I was thinking he was going to the bathroom but in fact when he reached me he punched me three times on the face! Surprised and startled I got up and grabbed a hold of his jumper and held him up against the wall. Yes, I did raise my voice along the lines of what do you think you are doing…only for the social workers to share this priceless piece of wisdom with me and I quote "Mr Gallacher if you don't stop shouting we will call the police and have you charged with breach of the peace" , Morag just sat there speechless and in shock. My reply was call them I have just been punched three times in the face and that is assault with what you allegedly took both boys into care with in the first place.

I repeated phone the police, at that they said Mr Gallacher let us all calm down and search for a way to resolve this. Again, my head was exploding if they had helped in the first instance, I would not be going back to the Spirit World without the Love of My Children and the Grand- children whom I have never met!!

Do I feel sorry for myself? no as below now follows the answers to the questions I have searched all my life…

All the answers are right in front of you which the divine has put in place for each one of us we just have to raise our awareness, and the answers will flow.
and Yes it is very difficult to understand at the time because as humans you automatically blame yourselves and think you are solely to blame for this and that and Yes it has taken you all these years separated from the ones You Love the most to understand it was never about You (me) it was to do with them facing their own challenges and learning lessons
which yes has impacted on you as an Individual but has also taught you many valuable lessons that enable You (me) to help others without looking for anything in return.

You All fight to hold on to what each one of you have but that is in fact the wrong thing to do, be it money or more Importantly each other because by doing so is counterproductive to each other as you stifle each other's spiritual journey this is why we must start to learn and more importantly understand every person that touches your life is a lesson or a blessing good or bad. We learn more about ourselves and evolve into better well- balanced loving, caring and compassionate people. That is the key that opens the soul to do what it has been sent here on its journey to learn. Playing with people's minds and their emotions hurts many!! instead of learning to let go and if they are to be part of your journey here on earth whatever the circumstances, they will find their way back to you. The only thing achieved playing with people's minds as if you own another human result in that person going on to mistrust and label everyone the same and that goes for both men and women. Your Mother and Father taught you many valuable lessons but to you the most important thing they taught you (me) was to be honest and truthful. They said if you are both these things people may not like you but they will respect you and you have followed that lesson successfully throughout your life and have handed it down to all your children. These are the very foundations that are now lacking in this world and that is why you feel deep within like an alien in a world you no longer understand but the one thing you realise is you (me) are not responsible for another person's journey. They alone have that personal responsibility and until you all get back to truly caring for each other this cycle can and will continue. That is why you all have yourselves major problems today instead of understanding each other and realising you come into this world with nothing and you will go out of this world the same way.

Embrace the lessons enjoy the journey understanding the truth about yourself first will allow you to love and forgive unconditionally and you will make the world a better place not only for yourself but more importantly for everyone's life that touches you in the course of your life time.

Morag and I grew closer together and we decided to get engaged. Both my sons started to drift back into my life and got to meet Morag and what was to become there Step Brother and Sister. But in reality, to me was in fact my children, another lesson learned that if you are not prepared to look upon step children as your children and that includes giving them direction in their lives then you may as well not get into a relationship.
Why do people use children as a weapon with each other and that includes our own children using the grandchildren against their own parents again "playing with people's minds and their emotions" resulting in grandchildren being split from their grandparents only based on their side of the story. Again, there is always three sides to a story… your side… their side… then the truth, and nine times out of ten as I stated earlier it is about taking personal responsibility and facing the truth about yourself and your own behaviour. This was another lesson on the horizon I was to learn and in such a dramatic way. I still struggle with my own child would come away with some of the things I am about to share and no, it is not to embarrass her or hurt her, as I also failed her as I could not take her pain away. I tried to give my own life so the three children would have their Mum, and if you met and knew Mary for whoever reads this you would begin to understand why I took the decision I took. Karen, when I tried to end my own life it was not because I did not love you or the boys or your Mum. I loved all four of you so much that in taking my own life after having a discussion with God and thus she would have been there for you all as you all needed Mum more than me.
This lesson is called unconditional love for those you truly love was God testing Me ? as I went through two fields in behind three hedge rows where you could not see the car from the road as it was hidden from view and then that was when I spoke to God in Truth for the very first time from my soul. I was pulled from the car and a "voice" said "you have work to do here" if I had tried this in a car park on a Saturday afternoon I could understand it, so it has taken me many years and lessons as this was just the first part of my journey here on earth, that has at times been so hard not having you and the boys in my life to hug and tell you that I love you all so much. I know the things you said was done in anger and for that I forgive you unconditionally and yes, I know by the time you read

this I will have returned home to the spirit world. And when it is your time to return home, I know you will understand everything that has happened and none of it was any of your fault.

As I said Morag and I got engaged in April 94, and planned a wedding for 1997 at Gretna Green. Six weeks before the wedding Karen and the boys were invited, but Karen said she would not be coming as she was not going to play happy families. I was not made aware that Karen phoned Morag six weeks before our wedding and said don't marry him he will batter you.
I was not aware of this conversation taking place and Morag only told me about a year later. I only discovered this after sitting in the house one night when I got a private message from someone called Amy, asking age, sex and location. I replied and still have on file today the conversation. I said I was a married man and had five children. It turns out it was my `own daughter` and again to this day I still don't know what was running through her mind.
The messages after she had let me know it was in fact her at that point Morag was aware as I hid nothing from her and that was when she shared the conversation she had with Karen before we were married. To be honest I was angry with Morag for not sharing that information with me, she replied "if I thought it was the truth I would not have married you"
Sometime later Karen again got in contact to accuse me of sleeping with her Mums friend who was slightly handicapped. I was stunned to say the least as I have never played with people's minds or their emotions and by that I have never said to any girl in my life I love you, just to get inside her pants and I would not cheat on Mary, another valuable lesson learned from my upbringing… treat others as you want to be treated yourself.

Morag had also made me aware that one of her family knew someone that lived close to where Mary and I lived. Apparently said to them, do not go out with Robert as he would beat her up!! A couple of years later the person involved turned up at my house as I was cooking Morag and I a steak which was a Friday night treat. He said to Morag I need to talk to Robert about a spiritual matter. God love her Morag said come in knowing full well that the steak would have to wait till I dealt with the problem they were encountering. It turned out he beat his wife and she had run away to a refuge. Here is the great thing when you genuinely can love and forgive a person unconditionally it lets your soul help someone on their journey. Spirit came forward and made him aware of the consequences of his action was part of the bigger plan that had already been worked out and he was told at that time he would meet a lady in a tartan skirt in a super market and told other stuff which I will not share with you. He laughed and said I will believe that when it happens! He left and it was steak time, it was delicious with onions and mushrooms and home cooked chips.

Both Morag and I ran into him funnily enough in a super market and he rushed over to tell me what I told him was the truth and they are together. I have not seen him since but hope he has learned his lessons and treats his new lady with respect as he has been given another chance. Gods plan is so subtle that once you become aware of his love for each one of us you become aware how much we are all part of the plan, it just takes your breath away!

I was contacted by my Sons wife, on Facebook and she said she had heard some awful stories about me and some good ones as well. To say this was a bolt from the blue is an understatement she explained that…

The children my Grand- Children were asking about my Sons Father their papa… Me! And she wanted to meet me first in Kilmarnock for a cuppa and a chat before introducing the children to me. I said you will need to speak to my Son and see if he is cool with that! She then contacted me to say that he had agreed it was time I met my Grandchildren. I was so excited and Morag was chuffed for me and suggested on the first visit I go myself in case they wanted to ask questions about their Gran (Mary)
I thought at the time how really understanding Morag was, so everything was arranged for me to meet them in a couple of weeks time, as they were going away. The days just dragged by and about two days before I was to meet them she got in touch to say Mark

was happy for me to see them, then the day after she got in touch to say he had blown up and did not want me to meet them. She was very embarrassed and kept apologising to me. I said it's not your fault and I have not heard from Mark or his wife since. The last I heard they had split up which is a shame as perhaps I could have helped them both look at things differently, but again it's all part of the plan I am not God and can't help everyone only those that want help I will be there for them, and that once again includes family.

Months passed and again right out of the blue my Daughter's girl got in touch with me via Facebook. Again I had never met her and only knew she would be a teenager at this point and again I have kept a transcript of the conversation.

She said I have wondered what you're like as I have heard bad and good things about you and would like to meet you. I never answered right away first I spoke to Morag and said do you really think this is my Granddaughter or in fact is it my daughter. She said reply but don't make any plans just thank her for getting in touch and if she wants to take it further perhaps a meeting then and only then I would have to make a decision. I did as Morag advised and a couple of days later she once again got in touch and said she would love to meet me. I said I don't have a problem with that but knew her Mother hated me with a vengeance as she sent me an e-mail that said I can't wait till your dead so I can come and see you in your box! Again, I have kept it hoping one day she would say I was and am so angry with you that Mum was taken and you have survived, which I understand her anger with me but it wasn't meant to be this way. Anyway, so I said I would meet up with her but it would be in an open place and Morag would be coming along with me but first she had to tell her Mum and if she was ok with her then fine no problem. I never heard anything for about three days and then she got in touch and told me she had spoken with her Mum and it was ok!! I sat in disbelief and said to Morag I will wait to reply tomorrow afternoon, that will give me a chance to take on the enormity of my Daughter forgiving me about not being able to save her Mum, as I said I would be there for them and protect them yet another valuable lesson learned.

Only God knows when it is your time here on earth and I can't and am not responsible for their Mums passing. I replied the next afternoon to her Facebook private message page, again I have the full transcript of the conversation but I have to add I honestly don't know why I was saving them. Anyway, as soon as I sent it she replied or what I thought was her in fact it was my daughter who said you will go to your grave without seeing any of the Grand Children. Don't dare contact my Daughter again. I replied it was her that contacted me and if she looked back on the messages, I said clear it with your Mum first I then added, this is your daughters private Facebook page and you should not be on it!!
I said I am not going to have a conversation with a child!
Morag seen the incoming messages and was so gob-smacked she went quite as she could see the pain in my face but this was to be insignificant in comparison to what was about to happen. Many months down the line Morag and I were invited to Morag's and my Son to his new flat. He had met a lovely girl and they fell in love and got a flat down by the shore together. We were both excited for them and the night duly arrived so we set off in the car down to their place we arrived they were so excited that Mum and Dad were coming they were at the window just as we pulled up, just at that my mobile phone went I answered it, it was my eldest Son saying Dad I have something to ask you and I know you will be very angry but I have to ask anyway. I sat there thinking in a split second what could he ever ask me that I would be very angry with what came out his mouth was then and to this day leaves me sick to the pit of my stomach and if you are reading this Karen I forgive you anyway but at the time I would have killed you if I got my hands on you… that is how angry you made me !!
Mark said did you rape Karen?
I had to ask him to repeat what he said as I could not believe what he just said. Morag saw my face turn chalk white and asked what was wrong, I said I will tell you in a minute.
I said Mark I would never do anything like that and I could not believe you have asked me that. He said I did not think you would do anything like that and rang off before I could say anything else.

I sat numb from head to toe all the while Morag saying what's wrong. As I was telling her the phone went again it was my youngest Brian who said, Dad Mark and me were with Karen last night and she said you raped her. I was livid with anger and I said Brian do you think I am capable of that? he said no but I have to ask as well, after I had repeated to him what I said to Mark. I followed it up by saying to Brian as soon as you go off the phone tell Karen to meet me at Kilmarnock Police Station at 9 am, "ok" I will Dad and he rang off.

I was shaking with anger and burst out crying with hurt. Morag said we will wait here till you have composed yourself Robert she shouted up to her Son we would be up in five minutes.
Just at that the phone went again I said to Morag go up and I will follow you up in ten minutes time. I answered the phone it was my late Wife's youngest Sister she said Robert Karen does not want to go to the police. I then said right we can both take a lie detector test and she said she won't do that either. I said well I will be going to the Police in the morning. She put the phone down and I went up to have a meal that they had taken the time and trouble to prepare for Morag and I.
Unfortunately, my mind was consumed with anger, hurt and disbelief that Karen even with all that she threw at me in the past would ever dream of saying such a thing!! I was gutted and burst out crying in front of my Son and his girlfriend. They had no idea what the matter was and joked the dinner was not that bad which made me cry even more as I had totally spoiled it for them and Morag. I settled down and we finished the lovely meal off and after pudding and a cup of tea we headed back up the road. I never spoke a word on the way home Morag made a cup of tea when we got home and I asked her if she would come to the Police Station with me first thing in the morning as by this time I had enough of Karen's carry on.

The next morning took forever to come as I lay awake all night trying to come to terms with "why" would she say that!!

The next morning Morag came with me to Saltcoats Police station where I asked to speak with an officer in a private room. Morag came in with me and just as I was sitting down the thought flashed through my mind about Mark telling the school I had punched his teeth out and me being charged with serious assault and knew again this was a test that I would fight and clear my name once again. After explaining to the Police officer what had taken place the night before he simply said until Karen makes an allegation we cannot intervene as it is only hearsay. I was appalled that someone can make an allegation against you without any proof.

Both of my Sons were to make me very proud as the morals and values Mary and I had installed in them had not been eroded even with everything that they had to cope with. The loss of their Mum, being taken into care, and all the other stuff they went through while in care, and the abuse they went through while in care which left me distraught that I had no control over as they were in my eyes taken into care illegally based on the fact that Mark had lied and even them knowing this they still pressed for a care order.

Anyway coming back to the meeting I had with the police, Morag and I left the station. I got a call from Brian to say both him and Mark were going to see Karen the following night. Two days later I got a call from Brian, he was very angry and once I had calmed him down he said that both he and Mark had questioned Karen about the allegation. When they asked when this happened, she replied with a date to which both boys said you were not in the house then. Now I have no doubt in my own mind that Karen has been raped... not by me but by someone else!!

Now if anyone else should read this please do not blame any of my children as I love and I am proud of them all. After all they went through, they have come through such a lot and hopefully each one of them are happier now and settled in their lives.
Brian was raging and wanted to go and kill her and I just said "Brian the power of the tongue is always more powerful than the fist"

He has not spoken to Karen since and my wish is on my death they can find some common ground to come together and be a family again as each one has suffered enough.

As for me, this was written to show each one of them that whatever they have done or said to me that it has not, nor will it ever kill the love inside me that burns for them every day.

I only hope this will meet with their blessing, that these events that are written down here are the truth and can be backed up with transcripts and my lawyer. I know this will help so many people to get answer's that will help them to come to terms with all the things that we as humans don't talk about, only to have lifelong regrets and pain with not being able to come to understand that everything in your life is for a reason.

But you must Learn the Lesson and move forward in your life.

Now let us look and explore death or the continuation of life as I look upon it.
I said I would discuss death, or continuation of life later, but at 38 years of age am I qualified to do so? You can be the judge.

The first experience of death for me was at a very early age, and although he was not related, the death of Mr Cook had a major impact on my life. I was confused, bewildered, I kept crying. He had committed suicide, why? No-one ever sat me down and explained to me about death, natural or unnatural. Yes, I knew Mrs Cook had left him. Yes, I suppose I saw a change in him as a person, but when you are young you invariably don't understand because you lack the knowing.

When the human form arrives here on the earth dimension it assumes that it will last forever.
It does not understand it has been designed for one purpose and that is to strengthen the soul and learn to understand that where it came from was a dimension of unconditional Love and Forgiveness
A place where love and Understanding only dwells. It is down to each individual to understand this thus working for the highest for each soul that enters their life.
For most though they will need to come back time and time again until they finally become aware and practice what the soul was sent here for.

I remember being very angry that I could not go to the funeral. To this day I still have not visited the grave in Ardrossan Cemetery (Update)… I visited the grave and was shocked and sad to see that he does not have any head stone or even a wee plaque to say he lived and died!! I approached the local priest in Saint Brendan's parish church which is now no longer there !, anyway I asked if funds could be made available for some sort of remembrance to him as I felt then and to this day the church was and should take responsibility for what was then and even now in my mind still is in a moral sense to acknowledge this man's life.
The response I got was… we don't have funds for that type of thing! Yes, but funds are available for your car, food and house! And, even after all these years, and having acquired the knowledge I was not responsible for his death or, if I had looked in the window and disobeyed my Mother that day, would I have saved him? The truth is I don't know the answer to that question.

Never at any time did someone sit me down and explain that death was a natural part of life. Yes, Priests told us Jesus was raised from the dead and he was going to prepare a place for all of us, but it was never fully explained that it was our spirit that went forward. Instead of instilling fear and hell fire and damnation to the extent you could not even talk to the Priest without being shouted at. It was so bad that when he did visit your home it was for reasons of not attending or putting a donation in the collection plate.

I remember one incident so very clearly that it was like only yesterday. The Priest came to visit our home early one evening and happened to go over to the table where my Brother's model aircraft were sitting. About six models were complete and on stands and one in progress of being made. He picked up the one that was being made, accidentally dropped it knocking two of the finished models off their stands, resulting in all three being damaged. Silence ensued, my Mother and Father not saying a word, my Brother, Sister and I sitting there gob smacked, not because he accidentally damaged the models but, more importantly, he never even said 'sorry' or even made an attempt to apologise.

When he left, I asked my Mum and Dad why they had not said anything. The just replied “Bobby you never question the Priest” Now, forgive me, you see as a young boy I was told never to question what the Priest said. I suspect I will not be the only person who grew up confused. As I said, that was my only encounter of death at that age.

Even then we were connecting to you to make you aware that the human frame is not to be trusted as it has its own agenda.
unless the soul that resides within is developed enough to know and understand that only unconditional Love and Forgiveness
then and only then will you All have a deeper understanding that it is only the Love and forgiveness your soul has given while in this human frame, as that is All that will return to the dimension from where it came.

A few years later I was to experience a different pain that I did not understand. You see my Brother had a friend called Brian Turner, a tall, slim, dark haired lad. Terry, my brother, and Brian went out to the local hotels and dance halls. Brian worked as a Telegram delivery person with the local Post Office. They enjoyed each other's company and got on very well together. I remember the two of them had just started a relationship with two girls and the two-some soon became a four-some, It was for me, being quite young, still amusing seeing Terry going through all the build up before it was time for him to meet his girl, and by that I mean getting bathed, ironing his own shirt, putting on all the good aftershave (I used to steal some after he left – he never knew that but he will now!).

This particular evening was special. The four of them were going out to celebrate Brian's 18th birthday. I remember Terry being quite excited about that particular evening, as they were going out for a Chinese meal and then onto the Laurieston Hotel in Ardrossan. The plan was Terry was to go to Brian's house and meet the two girls as Brian was working a wee bit late that evening, and as he smiled as he was going out the front door I just thought this is just another evening which seemed like any other, but obviously there was excitement in the air because he was going to meet a new girl and they were going out for a meal to celebrate Brian's birthday.

Anyway, I settled down with my Mum and Dad to watch tv. Everything was fine until later that evening. Terry came in earlier than expected and went straight upstairs. I sensed something was not right but did not know what. I went up to talk to him. He looked terrible and was crying. Brian never made it home.
He was killed on his last delivery coming back from West Kilbride.
The pain I felt for my Brother sitting on the bath crying I still cannot describe how hurt I felt for him. Terry changed after this. I think principally because no-one talked to him about death, I couldn't. I did not understand it either.

Years later, when I grew up and was going out with girls, I experienced a new set of painful lessons, the pain of splitting up. Again, part of growing up and learning lessons, how to deal with the pain, the rejection and there was a lot of rejection, primarily because you outgrow each other. I have still not figured out what is the difference between then and now. I am much older and, supposedly, wiser. Maybe you cope better when you are older or perhaps it is because when you are younger you don't experience the same fear of being on your own.

I experienced a sensitivity that at times I could not cope with. For example, on tv there was a programme called Lassie. remember the beautiful collie dog? Anyway, if she was hurt I would burst out crying which my Sister would make fun of and find amusing, and although I knew it was going to get better, well she had to as it was on the following week on TV, it still never altered the way I felt.

A few years later a neighbour four doors up from us passed away. I remember standing outside playing with my friend when a brown coffin was brought out from the house. At that point in my life I had reasoned in my own mind, as the neighbour was in her eighties, it was time for death, and yet as I sit and write this I feel even to this day there is never a right age to die because the intensity of the pain does not lessen with experience or age.

The next death that was to affect me greatly was my Gran in Stevenson. You see I spent a lot of time just sitting talking to her. We would spend literally hours and hours talking and then one day she was not there. As I sit and write this, again tears streaming down my face, I can still picture in my mind her sitting in her chair by the window and me sitting at her feet chatting away. I had to break off writing this and make myself a cup of tea. The pain has not diminished even after all these years.
This was just more than a lady I loved passing away, she was the rock of the Gallacher family and the very foundation the Gallacher family was built upon. I wait the glorious day when once again I can hold her in my arms and listen once again to all the stories she told me when I was a young boy.

My next encounter of death, or the fear of it, came one evening. I was being driven home by my fiancée's Mum Rena. We were chatting away. To me everything seemed normal. The next minute we found ourselves doing an emergency stop, a car on the opposite side of the road had crashed. Rena, after having done nursing most of her life, was first out of the car.

(I saw a different woman that night). Anyway, she was attending the injured. I was holding the front passenger's hand, a man with a football scarf on.
As I did not have any medical knowledge the only thing I could do was offer him comfort, reassurance. He had gone through the windscreen and had come back into rest in the seat. His head was burst open with blood everywhere and he was in shock and pain. He kept saying to me over and over again "I am going to die, I am going to die". I very quickly held his hand tighter and simply said with a conviction I found hard to understand, particularly as I was not a Doctor, but with such strong assurance "No you will not die, you will be okay" The ambulance crew arrived. Rena briefed them on what she knew and we continued on our journey. I remember being very quiet and Rena insisting she would come in with me. I had not long stepped in the house – my Mum and Dad were in bed asleep. Rena followed close by me as I went into the kitchen when suddenly I became static and burst out crying, it was delayed shock (for every action there is a reaction) and it was the delayed reaction to the road accident. No, it wasn't all the blood everywhere, it was hearing that man say "I am going to die". I suddenly thought how that man's family will cope. After several strong sweet cups of tea, I had calmed down. A good night's sleep followed.

Yes Robert you are correct in the sense that your love and experiences are all that returns home and yes you will all understand why this is so. It will amaze everyone that there is no mistakes or guilt of what has happened only lessons for the soul to develop.

The day after it was not given another thought. Strange though after all these years I can recall in such detail events I have experienced. It for me confirms what I have always known and that is when you die you take with you your life's experiences to be explored in greater detail.

Not long after this as I was coming back over from the shops and a man collapsed on the corner. A Doctor was called and as I stood there not knowing what to do and feeling helpless. The man was turning blue. The Doctor was taking ages, 20 minutes had passed and so had the man passed away with a heart attack. The small crowd that was there were waiting on a 'leader' (the Doctor) to help this man. I stood thinking to myself 'maybe we should all become leaders'. No, I don't mean Doctors, I mean helping each other. It was quite ironic that about 15 years later they started to publicise what to do in the event of a heart attack. You see we do learn lessons, albeit it takes years in some cases.

Throughout all these experiences I was quite honestly blind to the fact that life may in fact continue after what we know to be the physical death. Even today my mind still struggles with the concept of how we can possibly survive and yet an inner feeling that tells me yes, I will survive.

We have shown you through the healing and through the many messages we have passed through the human vessel that life does continue. The human mind is not equipped to understand that there are many dimensions, and realms awaiting the return home of the soul.

For me, as I told you earlier, my first encounter with the possibility that we do survive was when I attended the first clairvoyant evening with my Mum and Mary my Wife. Yes, it did throw me into total confusion and made me feel that all my life to that point had in reality been spent in complete and utter ignorance. That there was in fact a meaning, a purpose to life.

Now I have in my life been very lucky. I have given of myself my love, my help, unconditionally. At least for me it has given me great joy being able to reach out and touch someone's life and, after all, life is a two- way process. For the little I have given I have received in return so much more in terms of all the people that have allowed me to share in their experiences. And although I have to admit some have been very sad, even heart breaking at times, they have enriched my life so very much.

When I heard the medium talk to my Mum and knowing what she said was accurate, i.e. Bobby (me) represented you at the funeral as you were abroad on holiday, that the lady comes forward, she was a small lady who passed with a heart attack. That for me was the realisation there is a world behind the world we see. That was to be even more reinforced by the many messages I have received.

The one that changed my life completely and admittedly started to make sense to me as to why I have been so sensitive for all these years was a message from Sally Buxton and with this came this calmness I never thought possible.

When you have received a message or in fact many messages, I hope you quickly come to the realisation that there is a life after this one to consider. And the implications to that realisation is we must try very hard to change, not each other, but our own outlook to each other and how we change for the better ourselves, but more importantly, how we interact and care for each other as well.

Perhaps one day Spirituality may be taught. We would undoubtedly see a change for the better in our society.

One message I received from Albert Best, a Scottish medium, on May 10th 1993, in Kilmarnock Church. For me was and is the total assurance that yes life does continue. The message was as follows: -

1. A young lady comes forward with a memory of Skegness where you had a holiday together (fact).
2. The name of Fitzsimmons comes forward (my Mum's maiden name),
3. The names Willie (my Cousin Bill's father who is also known as Willie), Laura (Mary's aunt) comes forward from the spirit world as well.
4. The name Cherry, someone worked with coal with this name (Mary's friend Ann Cherry's son worked with coal).
5. Something wrong with one of the children's nose (Karen my daughter came back from the Sea Cadets with her nose badly sunburnt after being away on a weeklong rowing course),
6. Scar on your daughter's left knee (fact).
7. If I sit in the stillness, the quietness, I will hear the voice (this is still to happen), and finally
8. The name of Blair also comes forward (for me that was the final piece of unique evidence as the Undertaker's name who had attended to Mary was Mr Blair and in fact he also done my Mother's funeral as well).

Now, at this point I must say I am in no way trying to convert you or make you believe me. I cannot teach you anything, I can only make you think! Your belief will only come with your own personal circumstances and the proof you receive. But please, whatever you do, always remember that prior to going to a meeting or any meeting for that matter, always write things down so you may refer back to it or you may have to ask someone else about a piece of information, but at least you will have a record and a very detailed record of accurate information given to you at that particular meeting. Thus, saving you trying to remember some days and even weeks later. I would also like you to consider this.

The last experience I would like to tell you about does not make me feel proud, but as it happened not only did it happen, I was told about it in a message some 13 years later while sitting having a coffee with my friend Phyllis in my own home. I consider this last death/continuation of life story, not only mind blowing but again it reinforces the truth that there is life beyond what we can see at our point here on this earth. Anyway, this true story starts back in 1981. I had just joined Buckingham Toys which was part of the Ideal Toy Company, as a sales representative. My territory was all of Scotland and the North East of England. The job itself provided a challenge in as much the division I was working with up to that point of joining was dealing with the wholesale trade. My brief was to open new accounts but from within the retail sector. I was excited about not only joining one of the top five toy companies in the United Kingdom but the challenge that lay ahead of me. Mary, my wife, was also pleased as I had been out of work for some time and we were not getting on. The relationship was, in my eyes, in crisis. Mary just seemed to shut down but I thought it would come good again. As my area was large, I was away on business quite a lot of the week due to not only the territory size but because I was starting with no retail base which meant I had to cultivate it from scratch.

My sales manager, Chris Robins, was one of the most genuine sales people I have ever met. His gentle manner never detracted him from being professional. After my initial training Chris came up to Scotland, spending a couple of days with me on the territory to let him gauge, not only the response from the retail sector, but to him as equally important to meet my Wife. The three of us went out for a meal one evening and Mary took to him right away. That for me was one question answered that we would get along together and he would stand by you, very important in the selling industry.

Chris returned to his base and I carried out the task of opening-up new accounts. Things between Mary and I were getting steadily worse and my way of dealing with that was to work away a lot more.

I decided to concentrate my efforts in Newcastle by working there three days every week. My main objective being to open North Eastern Co-op, as the Sales Director and National Accounts Manager, as they could not make any headway, so I had a real challenge on my hands to get through the door and develop this account. I felt the key lay in developing this large prestigious account which would be very important to the company. Well, I called in every day as I was trying just to secure an appointment with the buyer, a gentleman called Terry Reid. He had quite a reputation as being not only one of the hardest people to see but also a very hard business man. Undaunted by this information, I kept leaving my business card until one day he was fed up with all the cards that were sitting in his tray. He told the receptionist that the next time I called he wanted to speak to me. This particular day the sun was out and I remember as it was so hot. I would call at the Co-op Head Office first as I was heading back to Scotland the same day. I walked in with a business card in my hand, I did not even have my sample case as I knew I would not get passed reception. The lady said "Take a seat Mr Gallacher, Mr Reid wants to speak to you on the internal phone". I was gob-smacked. I was called over and she said "You are now through to Mr Reid". His opening statement confirmed everything that had been said to me about him being a hard and difficult man to deal with. He said "Mr Gallacher, I am getting sick and tired of finding your business card on my table, what's your problem? It must cost your company a fortune to supply you with business cards". He then stopped. I replied "It does cost my company a fortune in business cards but that is only because you will not see me. The only problem Mr Reid I have is not being able to have ten minutes at your table to show you what our company has to offer you, and after the ten minutes are up, if there is nothing of interest to your company, I promise I will not disturb you again". His words are still resounding in my ears. He said "Right son, I like your style, you have got your ten minutes tomorrow afternoon at 4.30 pm sharp. Don't be late!" The conversation ended. Mr Reid just hung up the phone. I was worried about spending another night in Newcastle with regard to the expenses side of it for my company but as it had taken months of calling, I thought 'what the hell' for one more night.

I called ten minutes before my appointed time and with five minutes to go I asked the receptionist if she could advise Mr Reid, I was here for my 4.30 pm appointment. I went in with Mr Reid saying "You have ten minutes son, give it your best shot". Paul Latham tried and failed (Paul Latham being the Sales Director of the Ideal Toy Company). Still undaunted I went to three products I thought we could so some business on. "Right son, that's your ten minutes up, come and see me next Tuesday same time, I will give you an order for the three products you have suggested".
I was thrilled to bits.
The following week I picked up an order for their top eight stores. To say I was elated was an understatement. I quickly built up a rapport with Terry now having set up the background. This is where the story really begins.

One day while visiting Terry on a courtesy call he said "Here are two tickets for the Annual Co-op Dance". I said "I will only need one Terry as my Wife would not be able to come down at such short notice". Terry smiled and said "Come on Robert all you salesmen have girls while you are away from home, take the two". In order not to offend him I said "I will take the two tickets". The dance was being held in a club that joined the hotel I was staying in. I thought, brilliant, I can show my face, buy Terry a drink then disappear back to my hotel room. Well that was the plan.

The following evening came quite quickly. I went back to my hotel, washed, changed and went for dinner as there was 30 minutes to go before the doors opened. I decided to sit in reception with a glass of fresh orange juice and read a magazine. As I was sitting very relaxed, I was approached by a woman. She said "Excuse me can I ask a favour of you?" "Yes, how can I help you?" She explained she was waiting for a friend to come in. It transpires her friend worked at the North Eastern Co-op and they would be going to the dance and as she was frightened standing on her own could she sit with me until her friend arrived. I said "Of course, please sit down". We were chatting away quite the thing.

I then realised her friend was late and I would have to go in and show my face. I explained I would have to go in and said to her "If you want you can come in and sit with me until your friend comes". "My friend has the tickets" she replied. I said "No problem I have a spare ticket here".

So, we went in, we sat with soft drinks talking. I spoke to Terry briefly, more a nod really. He smiled as much to say 'I knew you had someone here Robert'. I thought I would let him think what he wants. The conversation with this woman went on. I am sorry I cannot tell you her first name because the truth is I have forgot and I feel really bad about that and as you read on you will find out why I feel so bad about not remembering her first name. Anyway, the evening wore on, her friend never appeared. By this time it was very late and she had missed her last bus. As I had my car downstairs in the car park, I offered to give her a lift home thinking that she stayed locally but in actual fact she stayed well out of the city in a place called Killingworth. I had found out quite a bit about her. She was an auxiliary nurse at the Freeman Hospital. She was divorced. Her husband was very abusive to her both physically and mentally.

We arrived at the flat, sitting in my car talking for a short while and I said I would have to go. "You will come in for a coffee Robert won't you?" I said "No, it's late". She insisted as she said it was the least she could do. She had such a wonderful time. I said "Okay" and duly went in and sat and had coffee with her. She disappeared while making the coffee and came back a short while later with a tray containing a coffee pot, a cream jug, and sugar dish, all in silver. I thought 'I would be happy with a mug of tea', Anyway, we sat chatting and as I was saying I would have to leave she then said to me "Robert I have had such a wonderful evening, can I see you again?" It would have been easy for me to lie at this point as Mary and I were not getting on, but in spite of that and because I loved Mary with all my heart I could not lie. I simply said "Look, I have had a wonderful evening too but I am married with three children". She looked at me and she burst out crying. She said "Robert no-one has ever been as honest with me as you

I respect you for being so honest Robert but please could I have just your friendship. There would be no harm in that surely" she said.

I said "Okay but there can never be anything other than friendship". She agreed and the friendship started. When I was down in Newcastle I would visit her and sit having a coffee and a chat. This went on for about three months. We would occasionally go out for a quiet drink, again sitting chatting away.

Over a period of time I got to know her and about her life. She had a terrible life with a man who never loved her. I sat thinking it was very sad that she never experienced happiness. On the way back from the country pub I put a tape in the car. It was Neil Diamond's Jazz Singer and I started to sing along to it. She said "You have a lovely voice Robert". I was embarrassed and said "No I don't really, I am not a good singer but I enjoy singing along as music is a great love of mine". She enquired what tape it was. I said it was the Jazz Singer. She said "That's on next week at the Cinema. I have always wanted to see that film Robert". I said "Well how do you fancy going next week when I come down?" and she said "That would be fantastic Robert, thank you so much. I said I would give her a ring and she said "Yes that's fine". I left to go back to my hotel. The following week arrived. When I arrived at the hotel the Corner House in Heaton, the assistant manager, I think his name was 'Tillie' although I can't be sure. Anyway, I had just checked in when he said "Robert there has been a woman with a local accent on the phone all weekend for you". I said "It's okay it is my friend, I will ring her later". I went and had a shower and to get changed. I tried to phone but it kept ringing out. I thought I will have my meal and then just drive up and see her as we were going to the cinema anyway. I finished my meal and headed up to Killingworth as I had done so many times before. I arrived at the flat. It was empty! I looked through the letterbox only to find one black bag sitting on its own in the middle of the floor. I thought to myself 'That's why she has been on the phone all weekend. She was moving to a new home and wanted to let me know'. I went next door to her neighbour who I never met before, chapped the door.

A lady appeared and before I could open my mouth she said "You must be Robert". I was slightly taken aback. I said "Yes, do you know where the lady next door has moved to?" She said "You had better come in and close the door Robert; I don't know how to tell you this". I duly walked in through the front door and closing the door behind me felt very cold. "She died over the weekend; the funeral takes place tomorrow Robert". I just stood there numb head to toe. "Her daughter wants to see you urgently Robert, she just lives over there" pointing to the flats directly opposite. I said goodbye and went to my car. I was sitting there numb and the tears just started streaming down my face. The neighbour came out and said "Come in for a cup of tea Robert". I said "No, I can't I will sit here for a moment then I will go back to my hotel". She spoke softly and said "Robert please go and speak to her daughter as she has been on the phone to me constantly asking if you have been yet. Please Robert". I said "Okay, I will go over". She pointed to her flat and gave me her house number, and off I went still numb and very upset.

I arrived at the door. I just stood there for five minutes as I had never met her daughter. I did not know what to expect. I took a deep breath and knocked on the door. A lady answered and said immediately "You must be Robert, come away in". Her Husband asked if I would like a coffee. I said "Yes please". Once he left the room I found myself blurting out "I promise I never touched your Mum, we were friends". She replied "It's alright Robert; my Mum told me all about you. The reason I wanted to see you was to thank you from the bottom of my heart". I sat looking at her puzzled. She went on "My mum has never experienced happiness in her life until you came along. "I have never seen my Mum so happy, I am so very grateful to you that before she died she experienced real happiness". I just sat there, tears streaming down my face thinking back to the previous week when I was thinking it was sad she had not experienced some happiness and yet here was her daughter telling me how happy I had made her Mum. To this day I cannot understand how I made her so happy. All I did was to sit and talk to her, listened to her, respected her and no I never at any point touched her.

For those of us that have tasted and experienced true happiness it is difficult for us to comprehend those that may have not and how lonely some people are.

I have tasted real happiness but know I am experiencing true loneliness. Yes, I have people round about me and I am truly grateful to God for that, but the loneliness I am feeling has taught me yet another valuable lesson and that is, when you have happiness don't take it for granted.

Loneliness is a human trait that makes the mind open to understand that each one of you have to go through it.
Thus enabling each one to understand the lesson that soul has just gone through
but more importantly for each one of you to learn the lessons that each person that touches your life is not necessarily for your benefit
but is part and the promise we the Divine have given each one of you in the human frame and that is each one will experience Love and Happiness in their Human form.

What you do with it depends on your own level of understanding and if you manage to not get caught up in the materialistic things and feel blessed in the simple things in life your journey here will be a success.

As I stated earlier, some 13 years later whilst sitting with a medium friend this event was relayed to me and I was told she met my Wife and she spoke to her.

God how I wish I knew what was said?

My only wish is that Mary will not hold this against me as I loved Mary with all my heart and soul. My only hope is Mary is aware of how much happiness, joy and pleasure I had received from her coming into my life.

All the events as detailed happened and if this helps one person to consider not themselves but others first… they will see their life change. Not only for the better but it will be beneficial to others.

Very lastly, I would like to mention the assistant manager of the Corner House as soon after this, he passed away in the cellar changing a keg of beer. I would like to raise my glass (cup of tea) to him and remember him as someone not only having a nice manner about him, he offered me comfort that night my friend passed away

I would also like to mention Chris Robins, my Sales Manager at Buckingham Toys. I was made redundant a few months after my friend passed away and sadly a few months later Chris passed away. If only he knew that, although he was my boss, and I respected him, I was very grateful to him for giving me an opportunity to work with one of the top five companies in the United Kingdom. But, more importantly, I was privileged that he touched my life.

Death is the ultimate of life but it can be made easier for the mind to cope with knowing that death is not the end but in fact is the continuation of life.

May God grant you happiness at some point in your lifetime.

One of my favourite story's that, describes perfectly the connection between us and the spirit world.

Once, in a little pond, in the muddy water under the lily pads, there lived a little water beetle in a community of water beetles. They lived a simple and comfortable life in the pond with few disturbances, and interruptions.

Once in a while, sadness would come to the community when one of their fellow beetles would climb the stem of a lily pad and would, never be seen again. They knew when this happened; their friend was dead, gone forever. Then, one day, one little water beetle felt an irresistible urge to climb up that stem. However, he was determined that he would not leave forever. He would come back and tell his friends what he had found at the top.

When he reached the top and climbed out of the water onto the surface of the lily pad, he was so tired, and the sun felt so warm, that he decided he must take a nap. As he slept, his body changed and when he woke up, he had turned into a beautiful blue-tailed dragonfly with broad wings and a slender body designed for flying.

So, fly he did! and, as he soared, he saw the beauty of a whole new world and a far superior way of life to what he had ever known existed.

Then he remembered his beetle friends and how they were thinking by now he was dead, He wanted to go back to tell them, and explain to them that he was now more alive than he had ever been before, his life had been fulfilled rather than ended.

But, his new body would not go down into the water. he could not get back to tell his friends the good news. Then he understood that their time would come, when they, too, would know what he now knew.

So, he raised his wings and flew off into his joyous new life!

~Author Unknown~

I honestly feel within, this is my last contribution, my last task here on earth (or is it? who knows, only the Divine has those answers)

But to be honest I have been blessed and privileged that so many people good and bad have touched my life.

Thank you all genuinely from the bottom of my heart and more importantly from my soul. As it has in its short time experienced many things but again, I have to acknowledge my part in all of this in as much as I came into this world with unconditional love and forgiveness and I am returning home the same way I came into this world

And finally, for my children, Karen, Mark and Brian, and NEVER forget this, I have and always will love you. I will watch over you.

Remember the key to success in life is to give your help, love unconditionally without ever looking for anything in return and God will watch over you, help you when you fail and comfort you when broken hearted.

Your Dad,

I love you.

Desiderata

Go placidly amid the noise and haste,
and remember what peace there may be in
silence. As far as possible without surrender
be on good terms with all persons.
Speak your truth quietly and clearly; and listen
to others, even the dull and the ignorant;
they too have their story.

Avoid loud and aggressive persons,
they are vexations to the spirit.
If you compare yourself with others,
you may become vain and bitter;
for always there will be greater and lesser
persons than yourself.
Enjoy your achievements as well as your plans.
Keep interested in your own career, however
humble; it is a real possession in the changing
fortunes of time.

Exercise caution in your business affairs, for the world is full of trickery. But let this not blind you to what virtue there is; many persons strive for high ideals, and everywhere life is full of heroism. Be yourself. Especially do not feign affection. Neither be cynical about love; for in the face of all aridity and disenchantment, it is as perennial as the grass.

Take kindly the counsel of the years, gracefully surrendering the things of youth. Nurture strength of spirit to shield you in sudden misfortune. But do not distress yourself with dark imaginings. Many fears are born of fatigue and loneliness.

Beyond a wholesome discipline, be gentle with yourself. You are a child of the universe no less than the trees and the stars; you have a right to be here. And whether or not it is clear to you, no doubt the universe is unfolding as it should.

Therefore, be at peace with God, whatever you conceive Him to be. And whatever your labours and aspirations, in the noisy confusion of life, keep peace in your soul. With all its sham, drudgery and broken dreams, it is still a beautiful world.

Be cheerful. Strive to be happy.

Max Ehrmann 1927

Acknowledgements

With special thanks to

Sally Davison and Linda Croxford

for their valuable and highly appreciated help in making my book become available to all.

Thank you for touching my life

DIANA

AND BEING PART

OF

MY JOURNEY

LOVE.

Casper

xx